Wokking Your Way

*dedicated
to food lovers who
are long on good taste
but short on
time*

to Low Fat Cooking

by Norma Chang

ISBN 0-9618759-1-7

Library of Congress Catalog Card No. 93-60859

Published in the United States of America by
The Travelling Gourmet
P.O. Box 911
Wappingers Falls, NY 12590

Manufactured in the United States of America
Printed by Tri-State Litho, Inc., Kingston, NY
Edited by Amy Wong
Cover design by Richard P. Chang

CONTENTS

INTRODUCTION

The American Dietetic Association, The American Heart Association, and the National Research Council all agree that for a healthier individual, no more than 30 percent of calories consumed should come from fat.

With this in mind it gives me great pleasure to introduce a low fat cookbook: *Wokking Your Way to Low Fat Cooking* by Norma Chang.

Chinese cookery has been for centuries a very healthy way of eating, but as with most cuisine, one has to be sensible in the amount of fat, the type of food, or meat one uses.

Low-fat does not necessarily mean low-flavor, and having sampled Norma's culinary delights for over twenty years, I believe her new cookbook will be a smash.

Connie Sung
Registered Dietitian

A NOTE FROM NORMA

It's not how much you eat, it's what you eat—and how you prepare it. I hope this book will help you to eat right.

Eating right does not mean depriving yourself of your favorite foods.

Eating a balanced diet does not mean eating boring meals or at the expense of your taste preferences.

Eating right and eating a balanced diet may require some modifications of your eating habits. It might seem threatening and sound like a lot of work, but it's actually easier than you think.

♡ Set a goal but do not try to achieve it overnight. Make gradual changes in your eating habits until your goal is realized. It may take weeks or even months, but the important thing is that you are working toward it.

♡ Eat moderate portions of your favorite foods. Balance a high-fat choice with low-fat choices.

♡ Eat a variety of foods from each food group. Choose food high in dietary fiber and low in dietary fat.

Be happy, eat well, stay healthy and energetic.

Norma Chang

BEFORE YOU BEGIN

☞ None of the recipes in this book is carved in stone. If a recipe calls for an ingredient that you cannot use—due to dietary restrictions, allergies, availability, or just dislike—feel free to omit it or make substitutions. Be creative! Like more vegetables? Decrease the amount of meat, poultry or seafood called for in the recipe or increase the vegetables, especially your favorite ones. Like lots of gravy? Add extra broth. Make cooking a fun experience.

☞ A spun-steel, carbon steel or cast-iron wok develops a patina through repeated seasoning with oil. This patina is what prevents woks made from these kinds of material from rusting. Spun-steel, carbon steel or cast-iron woks will not develop a patina without oil. Even the most well seasoned wok will eventually lose its patina from repeatedly cooking in it without using some form of fat.
When stir-frying without fat, I recommend using a stainless steel, non-stick, Calphalon or other rustproof wok.

☞ When a range is given for the amount of an ingredient to be used in a recipe, use the lesser quantity and increase according to taste. You can always add more if needed, but it is impossible to remove if too much is added.
The same applies to cooking time. Begin with the minimum time given, and increase according to need.

☞ Use the time given in a recipe as a guide only. Remember food at refrigerator temperature will take longer to cook than food at room temperature. Vegetables that are cooked as soon as harvested cook faster than vegetables that are less fresh. Young and tender vegetables require shorter cooking time than more mature ones. The amount of food in the wok or the pot and the type of equipment used also has an impact on cooking time.

☞ To prevent cross-contamination, after preparing raw meat, poultry and seafood always wash cutting boards, utensils, hands and all food preparation surfaces with hot soapy water immediately and sterilize.

BEFORE YOU BEGIN (continued)

☞ Always put food in clean dishes. Never put cooked food in the dish that held the raw meat, poultry or seafood.

☞ On a low-sodium diet? First try decreasing or eliminating the amount of salt called for in the recipe. If this still exceeds your total daily sodium intake, then decrease the amount of soy sauce called for in the recipe. This will satisfy a low-sodium requirement without sacrificing flavor.
To further reduce your sodium intake, drain and rinse all canned vegetables before using.

☞ On a low-cholesterol diet? In recipes calling for whole eggs, substitute 2 egg whites for 1 whole egg.

☞ When doubling a recipe, DO NOT automatically double liquid, salt, curry or other strong spices. Use your own judgment and taste as you go along.

TIME-SAVING TIPS

☺ Save dishwashing time: cut vegetables before meat, poultry or seafood.

☺ Freeze meat and poultry for 45 - 60 minutes to make slicing faster and easier.

☺ When cutting meats or poultry, slice or shred for more than one meal. Cook one family-size portion. Marinate another family-size portion to be used in a day or two. Package, label and date the other portions. Freeze for later use. No time to slice? Wash and trim meat or poultry. Package into desired portion and freeze. When you are ready to use it, partially thaw and slice according to the recipe.

☺ Set aside a time to do most, if not all, of the food slicing and preparation for the week.

☺ When cooking foods that freeze well, make extra for later use. Freeze in family-size or individual-size portions—great for those hectic days!

☺ Brown rice freezes well. Make extra for the freezer. Microwave to reheat.

☺ If carrots are used a lot in your household, peel extra and store in the refrigerator.

☺ For efficiency, when preparing food, place items to be sliced on the left of your cutting board, containers for holding sliced food to the right. Reverse the order if you are left-handed.

☺ Since adding oil to a preheated wok greatly reduces the chances of food sticking to the wok, I make a habit of placing my carbon steel wok on the cooking range, on low heat, as soon as I enter the kitchen to cook. The wok is preheated when I am ready to use it. This works for spun-steel, cast-iron and stainless steel woks too.

☺ Use a sharp knife. It will make the job faster and easier. A sharp knife also reduces the chance of getting cut, since it will do exactly what you want it to do.

TIME-SAVING TIPS (continued)

🕐 Save dishwashing time: marinate food in a plastic bag. Before adding ingredients, blow some air into the bag to make sure it has no holes. Measure marinade ingredients directly into bag. Close and shake to mix well. Add food, then press out as much air as possible. Close bag and shake to coat each piece of food with marinade. Place bag in a container (just in case there is a leak). Refrigerate till ready to use, turning bag occasionally.

DO NOT marinate in an aluminum container. DO NOT cover marinating food with aluminum foil; use plastic wrap. The acid and/or soy sauce in the marinade will react with the aluminum, resulting in an unpleasant metallic taste, as well as pitting the aluminum.

🕐 Stir-frying is a good way to accommodate the individual tastes of family members. Remove individual portions as they reach desired doneness. One wok satisfies many needs.

🕐 When planning a barbecue, think ahead. Plan more than one meal. First cook the current meal. Then put the future meal to cook on its own. Enjoy your barbecue, and look forward to some easy future meals.

Suggestions for future meals:

Baked Apricot Chicken, p.23

Chinese Roast Pork with Maple Syrup, p.164

Barbecued Maple Syrup Chicken, p.165.

KITCHEN HINTS

* Rub baking pans with lemon juice instead of oil to prevent food from sticking.

* Citrus fruits will yield more juice if brought to room temperature and rolled on countertop before juicing.

* To get seedless juice, wrap cut fruit with a piece of cheesecloth before squeezing.

* When using a fine grater to prepare citrus zest, to get more zest and to make cleanup easier, cover the grater with plastic wrap before grating. After grating, lift up plastic wrap and scrape off zest.

* Keep a quarter or half-teaspoon measuring spoon in the salt container for convenience in keeping track of sodium intake.

* Place a damp kitchen towel or paper towel under your cutting board to prevent the board from sliding when in use.

* To keep wax paper flat on countertop, wipe countertop with damp sponge before laying down wax paper.

* Keep a toothbrush in the kitchen for use in cleaning food (such as celery ribs) and utensils (such as garlic press and grater).

* Heating woks or other pots and pans before adding oil will help prevent food from sticking.

* A Dutch oven makes a good substitute for a wok or a frying pan.

* Snow peas look wilted? Soak in cold water for 15 minutes or more to freshen. This works for other vegetables too.

* Microwaved poultry and meat looking pale? Brush with a little dark or mushroom soy sauce.

* To accommodate non-chili eaters: when a recipe calls for Asian chili sauce, add it at the end of cooking after removing the non-chili eaters' portion.

* To prevent food from sticking to the barbecue grill rack, first

KITCHEN HINTS (continued)

preheat the rack, then brush with oil before placing food on the rack.

* To remove soy sauce stains from clothing or tablecloth, saturate stained area with hairspray immediately. Let stand for about thirty minutes then laundry as usual. Works for ballpoint pen stains too.

* Concerned about eating too much meat? Slice meat or poultry very thin. This makes portions appear larger than they really are, fooling the eyes as well as the stomach.

* To avoid spatters and make cleanup easier when pounding meat and poultry, place meat or poultry in one layer, leaving some room for expansion, in a freezer bag or other heavy plastic bag and pound away.

* When stir-frying vegetables of varying cooking times in the same recipe, give the vegetable that requires the longest cooking time the head start of a few seconds or minutes. Continue down the line, ending with the vegetable that requires the shortest cooking time.

* Dress up a dish with edible flowers (make sure they are free of pesticides or other chemical, DO NOT use flowers from the florist) like rose, nasturtium, violet, chive, Chinese kale, Chinese broccoli, or squash etc. Fruits like carambola, kiwi, berries, melons, blood orange or other citrus fruits also make attractive garnishes.

* Do not add kiwi or fresh pineapple to gelatin. They prevent gelatin from gelling.

* To prevent bamboo skewers from burning, soak skewers in water for at least 30 minutes before using them. Leave about a ¼ inch space between each piece of food to assure even cooking.

* Read my cookbook *My Students' Favorite Chinese Recipes* for more kitchen hints.

GINGER WINE

fresh ginger
pale dry sherry or sake or rice wine

❀   Peel ginger. Wash, pat dry and slice thinly.

❀   Place sliced ginger in a glass jar (or other non-corrosive container) with a tight-fitting lid. Cover with sherry, sake or rice wine. Keep up to 6 months in refrigerator.

Ran out of ginger wine? Not to worry. Just add the amount of wine called for in the recipe and a few slices of fresh ginger.

GRATING GINGER: Use a ginger grater, available at Asian markets. Or cover a fine grater with a piece of plastic wrap, peel and grate ginger, lift up plastic wrap, scrape off grated ginger and use as needed.

EXTRACTING GINGER JUICE: Pulverize a chunk of peeled ginger, using a mortar and pestle. If you don't have that equipment, smash a chunk of ginger with the flat side of your cleaver, place the smashed ginger in a cup or bowl, and use the handle of your cleaver to finish the pulverizing job. Add 1 - 2 teaspoons of water or pale dry sherry to the pulverized ginger, and work the mixture with your fingers to release all the ginger oil and flavor. Squeeze out as much of the liquid as possible. Strain if desired.

NOTE: Ginger and wine are two ingredients called for in just about all Chinese recipes.
Ginger is highly perishable, plus it always gets lost among the various vegetables in my refrigerator.
To save time and money, I decided to combine ginger and wine in a glass jar with a tight-fitting lid. Stored on the refrigerator door shelf, I know exactly where to find ginger and wine whenever I need them.

DRY-ROASTING NUTS & SEEDS IN A WOK

The wok can be used to roast any kind of nut or seed. If you are using a flat-bottomed wok, roast on low temperature and stir more frequently. If you are using the traditional round-bottomed wok, roast at medium to medium-low temperature. Once nuts or seeds begin to turn light brown, stir them frequently and keep your eyes on them as from this point on they will burn very easily.

❀   Preheat wok on medium for 2 - 3 minutes or till heated through. Lower heat to medium-low.

❀   Add nuts or seeds to wok (use no oil) and spread in a single layer. Stir-fry the nuts or seeds till a shade under desired doneness. Sesame seeds, and sliced and slivered nuts will take about 3 - 5 minutes; all other nuts and seeds will take about 10 - 20 minutes. Add 1 - 3 minutes more if nuts are at refrigerator temperature.

❀   Remove nuts or seeds from wok. Cool. Store in an airtight container.

NOTE: When roasting black sesame seeds, add a few white sesame seeds. When white sesame seeds are done so are the black ones.

POULTRY

17
Pine Nut Chicken with Three Peppers

18
Walnut Crusted Chicken with Mandarin Orange Sauce

19
Lemon Chicken
Baked Lemon Chicken

20
Chicken with Broccoli
Chicken with Cauliflower & Celery
Chicken with Brussels Sprouts
Chicken with Chinese Eggplant
Chicken with Green Beans

22
Crispy Apricot Chicken
Baked Apricot Chicken
Apricot Game Hen

24
Chicken in Black Bean Garlic Sauce
Chicken & Chinese Long Beans

26
Chicken & Asparagus Stir-fry
Moo Goo Gai Pan
Chicken & Bok Choy Stir-fry
Chicken with Cabbage
Chicken with Sugar Snap Peas
Chicken with Kohlrabi

28
Hoisin Chicken
Macadamia Chicken
Sesame Hoisin Chicken Kabobs

30
Turkey Pearl Balls
(Pork Pearl Balls)
(Beef Pearl Balls)

32
Sweet & Sour Lichee Turkey Balls
(Sweet & Sour Pork Balls)
(Sweet & Sour Lichee Veal Balls)
Sweet & Sour Turkey Kabobs
(Turkey Vegetable Soup)
(Turkey Noodle Soup)
Turkey Vegetable Stir-fry
(Spaghetti & Turkey Balls)

POULTRY RECIPES IN OTHER SECTIONS OF THIS BOOK

MONEY-SAVING, TIME-SAVING TIPS

Purchase extra chicken when on sale. Wash and pat dry. Trim and cut according to needs. Package in freezer bags or containers. Label and date.

Freeze at 0° or below.
You can keep: uncooked whole chicken, up to 1 year
uncooked chicken pieces, up to 9 months
uncooked sliced, diced or cubed chicken, up to 3 months
cooked chicken, up to 1 month.

Save chicken bones for making broth. If you are unable to make broth on the same day, freeze until time permits.

Boneless, skinless chicken breasts and thighs are now readily available at the supermarket. The price is higher, but it may be worth it when time is a factor to be considered. Stock up on these when on sale.

Turkey breasts can be substituted for chicken breasts in any of the recipes.

PINE NUT CHICKEN WITH THREE PEPPERS

1 pound boneless, skinless chicken breasts Remove and discard all
    visible fat. Cut into about ⅛" thick slices

2 teaspoons cornstarch
1 tablespoon ginger wine, p.13
1 tablespoon regular soy sauce
¼ teaspoon brown sugar

Combine. Add chicken. Mix well.
Chicken can be marinated the day
before and refrigerated.

1 medium red pepper Cut into about ¼" thick strips.
1 medium green pepper Cut into about ¼" thick strips.
1 medium yellow pepper Cut into about ¼" thick strips.
½ teaspoon kosher salt or to taste
1 teaspoon oil
1 tablespoon minced shallots
1 - 2 cloves garlic, minced
¼ - ½ cup chicken broth
2 - 3 tablespoons hoisin sauce
¼ cup pine nuts, toasted

❀   Add about 2 tablespoons broth to wok or frying pan. Bring to a
boil, using high heat. Add salt and peppers. Stir-fry till peppers are
heated through. Remove peppers and any broth to a plate and set aside.

❀   Add oil, shallots and garlic to wok. Stir-fry, using medium heat,
till shallots and garlic are translucent, adding broth a little at a time as
needed to prevent burning. Turn heat to high. Add chicken. Stir-fry
till chicken turns white, again adding broth a little at a time as needed
to prevent chicken from sticking. Stir in hoisin sauce.

❀   Add peppers. Stir-fry till peppers are heated through and chicken
is cooked, adding more broth as needed for gravy. Stir in 3 tablespoons
pine nuts. Remove to a serving platter. Sprinkle remaining pine nuts on
top. Serve.

Serves 4 - 6

WALNUT CRUSTED CHICKEN
WITH MANDARIN ORANGE SAUCE

1 ¼ pound boneless, skinless chicken breasts (4 halves) Remove and discard all visible fat. Flatten each piece with a mallet to even thickness.

1 teaspoon kosher salt or to taste
½ teaspoon sugar
white pepper to taste
1 tablespoon ginger wine, p.13
1 tablespoon regular soy sauce
1 egg white, lightly beaten

Combine. Toss with chicken to coat each piece well. Marinate 1 hour at room temperature or overnight in the refrigerator.

1½ - 2 cups walnuts Chop finely (to the size of rice grains).
1 15-ounce can mandarin oranges Drain. Reserve liquid.

Juice from mandarin oranges
2 tablespoons rice vinegar
2 teaspoons sugar
2 teaspoons regular soy sauce
¼ - ½ cup chicken broth

Combine in a small saucepan. This is the mandarin orange sauce.

1 tablespoon cornstarch
2 tablespoons water

Combine. Stir before adding to saucepan.

❀　Coat chicken pieces well with chopped walnuts. Place on a baking pan brushed with lemon juice or a non-stick baking pan.

❀　Bake uncovered, in the middle of the oven, at 425°F for 12 - 15 minutes or until done. Arrange on serving platter.

❀　Bring mandarin orange sauce to a boil. Thicken with cornstarch mixture. Gently stir in drained mandarin oranges. Spoon over baked chicken. Serve.

Serves 4

LEMON CHICKEN

1¼ pounds boneless, skinless chicken breasts (4 halves) Remove and
discard all visible fat. Flatten each piece with a mallet to even
thickness.

1 teaspoon kosher salt
½ teaspoon sugar
dash of white pepper or to taste
1 tablespoon cornstarch
1 tablespoon ginger wine, p.13

Combine. Add chicken. Toss to
coat each piece well. Marinate
½ hour at room temperature or
overnight in the refrigerator.

2 tablespoons sugar
1 tablespoon cornstarch
2 tablespoons fresh lemon juice
1 tablespoon regular soy sauce
3 tablespoons catsup
½ - 1 cup water

Combine in a frying pan large
enough to hold chicken in one
layer. This is the sauce.

❀   Using medium heat, bring ingredients in frying pan to a boil,
stirring constantly. Add marinated chicken. Return to a boil. Cover
pan. Lower heat to medium low. Cook chicken 5 - 8 minutes or till
done.

❀   Remove chicken to serving platter. Spoon sauce over chicken.
Serve with lots of rice.

Serves 4

VARIATION ON THE THEME

BAKED LEMON CHICKEN

Substitute: *3 - 4 pounds skinless chicken drumsticks* for the *chicken
breasts.*
❀   Double marinating ingredients. Bake at 350ºF, uncovered, for
45-60 minutes. Measure sauce ingredients into a small saucepan.
Bring to a boil, stirring constantly. Pour over baked chicken.

CHICKEN WITH BROCCOLI

1 pound boneless, skinless chicken breasts Remove and discard all
   visible fat. Cut into about ¼" thick slices.

1 tablespoon cornstarch
1 teaspoon sugar
2 tablespoons ginger wine, p.13
1 tablespoon regular soy sauce
1 - 2 tablespoons oyster sauce
¼- 1 teaspoon Asian chili sauce
¼ teaspoon white pepper

Combine. Add chicken. Mix
well. Marinate ½ hour at room
temperature or overnight in
the refrigerator.

1 - 1½ pounds broccoli Cut florets into bite-sized pieces. Peel
   stems and slant-cut into bite-sized pieces. Place all the broccoli
   in a large container. Cover with boiling water. Stir. Drain. Cool
   under cold running water. Drain well.
1 carrot, peeled and slant-cut
1 onion, about 4 - 6 ounces, cut into 6 or 8 lengthwise wedges
1 - 2 teaspoons minced garlic or to taste
¾ - 1 cup chicken broth
1 teaspoon oil
½ teaspoon kosher salt or to taste

❀   In a wok or large frying pan, bring ¼ cup broth to a boil, using
high heat. Add broccoli, carrot and onion. Stir-fry till vegetables are
slightly under desired doneness, about 3 minutes for crisp-tender.
Remove vegetables and any remaining broth to a platter.

❀   Add oil and garlic to wok. Stir-fry, using medium heat, till garlic
is lightly browned. Add ½ cup broth. Bring to a boil using high heat.
Add chicken. Stir-fry till chicken is cooked, about 3 - 5 minutes. Stir
in vegetables and additional broth as needed for gravy. Add salt to
taste. Serve.

Serves 4 - 6

Variations on the Theme

Chicken with Cauliflower & Celery

Substitute: *1 pound cauliflower* and *2 - 3 ribs celery* for the *broccoli*. Cut cauliflower into bite-sized pieces. Slant cut celery into about ½" thick slices.

Chicken with Brussels Sprouts

Substitute: *1 - 2 pounds Brussels sprouts* for the *broccoli*. Trim off mature leaves. Cut small sprouts in halves, large ones in quarters.

Chicken with Chinese Eggplant

Substitute: *1 - 1¼ pounds Chinese eggplant* for the *broccoli*. Remove and discard eggplant caps. Cut eggplant in half, lengthwise, then slant-cut into about ¼" thick slices.

Chicken with Green Beans

Substitute: *1 - 1¼ pounds green beans* for the *broccoli*. Remove ends and strings from beans. Cut into shorter sections if desired.

CRISPY APRICOT CHICKEN

3½ - 4 pounds chicken legs (drumsticks) Remove and discard skin and all visible fat. Rinse and pat dry.

1 teaspoon kosher salt
3 tablespoons apricot jam
2 tablespoons rice vinegar
2 tablespoons ginger wine, p.13
1 tablespoon mushroom soy sauce
1 -2 tablespoons regular soy sauce
2 cloves garlic, peeled
¼ teaspoon white pepper

Combine. Purée, using food processor or blender. Add to chicken. Mix well. Marinate ½ hour at room temperature or overnight in the refrigerator.

2 cups crispy rice cereal, crushed
2 tablespoons black or white
  sesame seeds (optional)

Combine in a pie plate or on a piece of wax paper. This is the coating.

2 teaspoon cornstarch
1 tablespoon water

Combine in a small dish. Stir before adding to saucepan.

❀ Remove chicken from marinade (reserve the marinade). Coat each piece well with crispy rice and sesame seed mixture. Place on a baking pan brushed with lemon juice or a non-stick baking pan.

❀ Bake uncovered, in the middle of the oven, at 425°F for 30 minutes. Turn off oven. Allow chicken to remain in warm oven for 5 minutes. Arrange cooked chicken on serving platter.

❀ Pour reserved marinade in a small saucepan. Add ½ cup water. Bring to boil. Thicken with cornstarch mixture. Strain in a sauce dish. Serve with chicken.

Serves 4 - 6

VARIATIONS ON THE THEME

BAKED APRICOT CHICKEN

Substitute: *1 whole 3½ - 4 pound chicken* for the *chicken legs.*
        Marinate overnight in the refrigerator.

❀   DO NOT coat chicken with crispy rice and sesame seed mixture.

❀   Bake at 375°F for 1¼ - 1¾ hours or till done. Remove skin before serving.

❀   OR: Grill for 1¼ - 1¾ hours or till done, turning once or twice.

APRICOT GAME HEN

Substitute: *3 Cornish game hens (weighing about 1¼ pounds each)* for the *chicken legs.*
        Cut each hen in half. Remove and discard skin and all
        visible fat. Marinate overnight in the refrigerator.

❀   Coat with crispy rice and sesame seed mixture. Bake at 425°F for 30 - 45 minutes, or till done.

❀   OR: DO NOT coat with crispy rice and sesame seed mixture. Grill for 40 - 50 minutes or till done, turning once or twice.

CHICKEN IN BLACK BEAN GARLIC SAUCE

1 pound boneless, skinless chicken breasts Remove and discard all
visible fat. Cut into about ¼" thick slices.

1 tablespoon cornstarch *2 tablespoons ginger wine, p.13* *1 tablespoon oyster sauce* *1 tablespoon mushroom soy sauce* *1 teaspoon sugar* *¼ teaspoon white pepper or to taste*	Combine. Add chicken. Mix well. Marinate 1 hour at room temperature or overnight in the refrigerator.

1 - 2 cups shredded romaine or iceberg lettuce
3 - 5 scallions Cut into about 1" lengths.
1 cup red pepper strips (about the same size as scallions)
½ - 1 teaspoon oil
1½ tablespoons fermented black beans Rinse and drain.
1 tablespoon minced garlic or to taste
1 teaspoon grated fresh ginger or to taste
¼ - 1 teaspoon Asian chili sauce or to taste (optional)
1 - 1½ cups chicken broth

❀   Line a serving platter with shredded lettuce.

❀   Heat wok. Add oil, fermented black beans, garlic, ginger and
chili sauce. Stir-fry over medium heat till fragrant, 2 - 3 minutes,
adding broth 1 tablespoon at a time, if wok seems dry, to prevent
burning.

❀   Add 1 cup broth to wok. Bring to a boil, using high heat. Boil
1 - 2 minutes to infuse. Add scallion and chicken. Stir-fry till
chicken is cooked. Stir in red pepper and additional broth as needed
for gravy. Spoon over lettuce and serve.

Serves 3 - 4

VARIATIONS ON THE THEME

Instead of *lettuce*, line platter with any of the following:

1 pound spinach, leaves and stems Cut in 2 or 3 pieces if desired.
❀   Blanch in broth or water for 1 minute. Drain well.

1 - 2 bunches watercress, leaves and stems Cut into shorter lengths if
   desired.
❀   Blanch in broth or water for 1 - 2 minutes. Drain well.

1 pound bean sprouts
❀   Blanch in broth or water for 30 seconds. Drain well. Elevate bean
sprouts to a higher plateau by removing the head (bean) and tail (root)
of each sprout before blanching. In Chinese, these headless and tailless
bean sprouts are called "silver needles."

1 - 2 pounds Vidalia onions
❀   Slice thinly. Stir-fry in 2 - 3 tablespoons broth till desired doneness is reached.

1 bunch Chinese parsley
❀   Wash and dry well.

CHICKEN & CHINESE LONG BEANS

Add: *½ - 1 pound Chinese long beans.* Cut into about 2" lengths.
Eliminate: *lettuce.* There is no need to line platter.
❀   Heat wok. Add oil, fermented black beans, garlic, ginger and
chili sauce. Stir-fry over medium heat till fragrant, 2 - 3 minutes,
adding broth 1 tablespoon at a time, if wok seems dry, to prevent
burning. Turn heat to high. Add beans. Stir-fry till beans are slightly
below desired doneness, 5 - 8 minutes for crisp-tender beans, adding
broth if wok seems dry to prevent burning. Remove to platter. Go to
the last step in the recipe at left. Stir in long beans at the same time
as red pepper. Transfer to serving platter. Serve.

CHICKEN & ASPARAGUS STIR-FRY

1 pound boneless, skinless chicken breasts Remove and discard all
 visible fat. Cut into about ¼" thick slices.

1 tablespoon cornstarch *½ teaspoon kosher salt or to taste* *1 teaspoon sugar* *1 tablespoon ginger wine, p.13* *1 tablespoon regular soy sauce* *white pepper to taste*	Combine. Add chicken. Mix well. Marinate ½ hour at room temperature or overnight in the refrigerator.

1 - 2 pounds asparagus Peel (see note), remove scales, slant-cut.
½ - 1 cup carrot slices
1 teaspoon kosher salt or to taste
¾ - 1 cup chicken broth
1 tablespoon oyster sauce (optional)

❀   In a wok or large frying pan, bring 2 tablespoons broth to a boil,
using high heat. Add asparagus and carrot. Stir-fry till asparagus
changes color. Remove vegetables to a platter, leaving broth in wok.

❀   Add ½ cup broth to wok. Bring to a boil, using high heat. Add
chicken. Stir-fry till chicken is cooked, adding more broth as needed
for gravy. Stir in vegetables and oyster sauce.

NOTE: Peeling asparagus makes the whole spear usable. With a
sharp paring knife, start peeling at the root end to about ¼ - ½ of the
length of the spear.

Serves 4 - 6

VARIATIONS ON THE THEME

CHILI LOVERS: Add *Asian chili sauce* or *Asian chili garlic sauce*
                        to taste any time during cooking.

CHICKEN & ASPARAGUS STIR-FRY (continued)

MOO GOO GAI PAN (Chicken with Fresh Mushrooms)

Substitute: *8 - 12 ounces sliced fresh mushrooms and 4 - 6 ounces snow peas* for the *asparagus*.
Remove ends and strings from snow peas.

CHICKEN & BOK CHOY STIR-FRY

Substitute: *1 - 2 pounds bok choy* for the *asparagus*.
Slant-cut bok choy into about ½" pieces.
NOTE: Because of the high water content of bok choy, you will need extra cornstarch and water to thicken sauce.

CHICKEN WITH CABBAGE

Substitute: *1 - 2 pounds green cabbage* or *Savoy cabbage* for the *asparagus*.
Cut cabbage into about ½" strips.

CHICKEN WITH SUGAR SNAP PEAS

Substitute: *8 - 12 ounces sugar snap peas, 1 cup yellow pepper strips and 1 8-ounce can sliced water chestnuts* for the *asparagus*.
Remove ends and strings from sugar snap peas.

CHICKEN WITH KOHLRABI

Substitute: *3 - 4 kohlrabi, ½ cup sliced bamboo shoots, and 1 medium onion* for the *asparagus*.
Peel kohlrabi and cut to about the same size as bamboo shoots.
Cut onion lengthwise into 4 - 6 wedges.

HOISIN CHICKEN

1 pound boneless, skinless chicken breasts Remove and discard all
    visible fat. Cut into about ¾" cubes.

1 tablespoon cornstarch
1 tablespoon ginger wine, p.13
1 tablespoon regular soy sauce
2 - 3 tablespoons hoisin sauce
¼ teaspoon kosher salt or to taste

Combine. Add chicken. Mix
well. Marinate ½ hour at room
temperature or overnight in
the refrigerator.

1 medium green pepper
1 medium red pepper

Cut into about 1" squares.

1 8-ounce can sliced water chestnuts, drained
¾ - 1 cup chicken broth
kosher salt to taste
¼ - ½ cup sliced almonds, toasted

❀   In a wok or large frying pan, bring 2 tablespoons broth to a boil,
using high heat. Add peppers and water chestnuts. Stir-fry till peppers are heated through. Remove vegetables to a platter, leaving
broth in wok.

❀   Add ½ cup broth to wok. Bring to a boil, using high heat. Add
chicken. Stir-fry till chicken is nearly cooked, 3 - 4 minutes, adding
more broth as needed for gravy. Add vegetables. Stir-fry till chicken
is cooked and vegetables reached desired doneness, 2 - 3 minutes.
Add salt to taste. Transfer to serving platter. Sprinkle toasted
almonds on top. Serve.

Serves 4 - 5

TOAST ALMONDS in a clean, dry wok or frying pan (use no oil)
over medium heat, 3 - 5 minutes, or till lightly browned, stirring
frequently. Or bake in a shallow baking pan at 300°F, 3 - 6 minutes,
stirring once or twice. Cool and store in an airtight container, if not
using at once. Will keep up to 1 week.

Variations on the Theme

Macadamia Chicken

Substitute: *¾ cup sliced bamboo shoots* and *½ cup straw mushrooms*
        for the *water chestnuts*
        ¼ - ½ cup macadamia nuts for the *almonds*.
❀   Stir in macadamia nuts instead of sprinkling on top.

Sesame Hoisin Chicken Kabobs

Reduce: *cornstarch* to 1 teaspoon.
Substitute: *8 - 10 ounces small mushrooms* or *large ones cut in halves*
        or quarters for the *water chestnuts*
        toasted sesame seeds for the *sliced almonds*.
Add: *1 can baby corn*. Cut each ear of corn into 2 or 3 pieces.

Add to chicken broth: *1 teaspoon Asian sesame oil or to taste*
        1 tablespoon hoisin sauce
        1 tablespoon cornstarch.
❀   Combine in a small saucepan. Bring to a boil, stirring constantly.
This is the sauce.

8" - 12" bamboo skewers. Soak in water at least 30 minutes to prevent
        burning.

❀   Thread marinated chicken on bamboo skewers, alternating
chicken cubes with green peppers, red peppers, mushrooms and baby
corn. Brush with sauce.
❀   Broil in middle of oven or grill 6 - 10 minutes or till done, turning
occasionally. Sprinkle sesame seeds on top. Serve.

TURKEY PEARL BALLS

1 pound ground turkey
3 large Chinese dried mushrooms Soak in warm
    water ½ hour to soften. Discard stems. Finely
    chop caps.
2 tablespoons finely chopped water chestnuts
1 small onion, finely chopped
1 egg, lightly beaten
1½ teaspoons kosher salt or to taste
¼ teaspoon sugar
dash white pepper or to taste
1 tablespoon ginger wine, p.13
1 tablespoon regular soy sauce

Combine well.
Can be done the
day before and
refrigerated.

1 cup glutinous rice Soak 2 - 3 hours. Drain well before using.

¼ - 2 teaspoons Asian chili sauce
2 tablespoons regular soy sauce
2 tablespoons rice vinegar or to taste

Combine in a small serving
dish. This is the dipping
sauce.

1 - 2 pounds napa cabbage, shredded

❧ Add water to steamer base. Line steamer basket or steamer rack
with napa cabbage. Cover. Bring to a boil. Steam (see p.186) for 3 -
5 minutes to soften cabbage a bit.

❧ Gently shape turkey mixture into balls, using about 1 tablespoon
mixture for each ball. Roll in drained rice to coat completely.

❧ Arrange turkey balls on top of steamed cabbage, leaving a little
space between each. Steam, covered, over high heat for 30 minutes.
Serve with dipping sauce.

Serves 4 - 6

NOTE: Overmixing turkey mixture and overrolling pearl balls will
result in a dense finished product. Give the mixing and rolling a
light touch!

TURKEY PEARL BALLS (continued)

Pearl balls freeze well. Make extra for the freezer. To freeze:

Method 1. Package cooked and cooled pearl balls into individual- or family-size portions. Label, date and freeze.

Method 2. Arrange cooked and cooled pearl balls in a single layer in a flat container, lined with plastic wrap, or a foam tray, leaving a little space between each pearl ball (this will make it easier to thaw the exact amount needed). Cover with a double thickness of plastic wrap, arrange another layer of pearl balls on plastic, repeat if necessary. Wrap, label, date and freeze. Will keep up to 2 months.

SERVING SUGGESTION

Make smaller pearl balls, using about 1 teaspoon of mixture for each ball. Serve as a first course at a dinner party or serve as hors d'oeuvres at a cocktail party.
If making smaller pearl balls, soak additional rice (1½ - 2 cups) since there will be more surface to be covered with rice.

VARIATIONS ON THE THEME

PORK PEARL BALLS

Substitute: *1 pound lean ground pork* for the *ground turkey.*
Add to pork mixture: *2 tablespoons chopped carrots*
1 teaspoon oyster sauce.

BEEF PEARL BALLS

Substitute: *1 pound very lean ground beef* for the *ground turkey*
½ cup mashed boiled potatoes for the *water chestnuts.*
Add to the beef mixture: *1 - 2 tablespoons finely chopped Chinese parsley*
1 - 2 teaspoons oyster sauce.

Sweet & Sour Lichee Turkey Balls

1 pound ground turkey
1 egg, lightly beaten
¼ cup flour
1 tablespoon ginger wine, p.13
1 tablespoon regular soy sauce
2 tablespoons minced shallots
½ teaspoon kosher salt
dash white pepper or to taste

Combine well. Form into 1" balls. Place on baking pan brushed with lemon juice or a non-stick baking pan. Bake at 350°F for 20 - 25 minutes. This can be done the day before.

2 tablespoons sugar or to taste
1 tablespoon ginger wine, p.13
2 tablespoons white vinegar or to taste
¼ cup tomato sauce
¼ cup regular soy sauce
liquid from can lichees combined with
* water to make ½ cup liquid*

This is the sauce. Combine in a saucepan large enough to accommodate vegetables and turkey balls.

1 carrot Peel and cut into about ¼" thick slices.
½ cup sliced bamboo shoots
1 large onion Cut into chunks.
1 20-ounce canned lichee Drain and reserve liquid.
½ - 1 green pepper Cut into about 1" square pieces.

1½ tablespoons cornstarch
2 tablespoons water

Combine in a small dish. Stir well before adding to saucepan.

❀   Over high heat, bring sauce to a boil. Add carrot, bamboo shoots and onion. Cook till vegetables are slightly under desired doneness.

❀   Add meatballs, lichees and green pepper. Bring to boil. Cook till meatballs are heated through. Thicken sauce with cornstarch mixture.

Serves 4 - 6

Turkey Balls freeze well. Make extra for the freezer.

Variations on the Theme

Sweet & Sour Pork Balls

Substitute: *1 pound lean ground pork* for the *ground turkey*
          ¼ cup cornstarch for the *flour*
          1 8-ounce can pineapple chunks for the *lichees*.

Sweet & Sour Lichee Veal Balls

Substitute: *1 pound ground veal* for the *ground turkey*
          ¼ cup tapioca starch for the *flour*.

Sweet & Sour Turkey Kabobs

8" - 12" bamboo skewers Soak in water 30 minutes to prevent burning.
❀   Combine sauce in a small saucepan. Bring to a boil. Simmer till sugar is dissolved. Thicken with cornstarch mixture.
❀   Thread turkey balls on bamboo skewers, alternating with vegetables. Brush with sauce. Broil or grill to desired doneness, turning and brushing with sauce occasionally.

Turkey Vegetable Soup

Bring: *chicken broth* to boil.
Add: cooked *turkey balls* and *vegetables* of choice.
❀   Return broth to a boil. Simmer till turkey balls are heated through and vegetables reach desired doneness.

CHILI LOVERS: Add *Asian chili oil* or *Asian chili sauce* to taste.

Turkey Noodle Soup

Add: cooked *noodles* and rinsed *Szechuan preserved vegetables* to taste (optional), to Turkey Vegetable Soup above.

SWEET & SOUR LICHEE TURKEY BALLS (continued)

TURKEY VEGETABLE STIR-FRY

Stir-fry: *vegetables* of choice.
Add: cooked *turkey balls* and *chicken broth* or *water* if you want
    gravy.
Stir in: *oyster sauce* to taste when turkey balls are heated through
    and vegetables reach desired doneness.
Thicken with: *cornstarch and water mixture* as needed.

SPAGHETTI & TURKEY BALLS

Add: cooked *turkey balls* to *marinara sauce* and serve over cooked
    spaghetti.

PORK, VEAL & LAMB

MONEY-SAVING, TIME-SAVING TIPS

When a recipe calls for sliced pork, using boneless pork loin chops makes the job faster and easier. However, when a recipe calls for shredded pork, it is better to begin with a whole piece of meat. Freezing the meat for 45 - 60 minutes will make shredding and slicing much easier.

Some leaner cuts of pork include: loin roast, loin chop, sirloin, tenderloin and shoulder.

Freeze at 0° or below.
You can keep: uncooked roast, up to 8 months
               uncooked chops, up to 4 months
               uncooked ground pork, up to 4 months
               cooked pork, up to 3 months.

Making your own ground pork is very easy, and if you have a food processor it is a snap. Trim away all visible fat from the pork, and cut into 1" cubes. Place in food processor bowl, about a ½ pound at a time; pulse till desired texture is reached. There are many advantages to making your own ground pork. Besides saving money, you have control over the fat content and the texture of your ground pork.

If you are unable to consume pork due to health or dietary restrictions, substitute veal or turkey for the pork in any of these recipes. I have given some suggestions as a reminder.

Sesame Teriyaki Tenderloin

1 - 1¼ pound pork tenderloin Remove and discard all visible fat.

1 tablespoon brown sugar *2 tablespoons ginger wine, p.13* *3 tablespoons teriyaki sauce* *4 - 8 cloves garlic,* crushed *2 - 3 scallions* crushed *kosher salt to taste* *white pepper to taste*	Combine in a heavy plastic bag. Add tenderloin, coat with mixture. Press out as much air as possible. Seal bag. Marinate 2 hours or overnight in the refrigerator.

½ cup pork or chicken broth
½ teaspoon Asian sesame oil (optional)
1 - 2 tablespoons toasted sesame seeds
green and white scallion rings for garnish

2 teaspoon cornstarch *1 tablespoon water*	Combine in a small dish. Stir well before adding to sauce.

❀ Remove tenderloin from marinade. Place on a rack in a shallow baking pan. Bake at 400°F for 25-35 minutes or till meat thermometer registers 160°F. Slice thinly and arrange on serving platter.

❀ Pour marinade into a small saucepan. Add broth. Bring to a boil. Thicken with cornstarch mixture. Stir in sesame oil. Spoon over sliced tenderloin. Sprinkle sesame seeds and scallion rings on top. Serve.

Serves 4 - 6

Variation on the Theme

Sesame Teriyaki Pork Chops

Substitute: *Lean pork loin chops* for the *tenderloin.*
❀ Broil in the middle of the oven, 6 - 7 minutes on each side.

PORK WITH FERMENTED BLACK BEANS

1 pound lean boneless pork loin Remove and discard all visible fat. Slice thinly (about 2"× ½"×⅛").

1 tablespoon cornstarch
2 tablespoons ginger wine, p.13 Combine. Add pork. Mix well.
1 tablespoon oyster sauce Marinate ½ hour at room
1 tablespoon mushroom soy sauce temperature or overnight in
1 teaspoon sugar refrigerator.
white pepper to taste

1 - 2 pounds napa cabbage Cut lengthwise into ½" wide strips. Cut strips into about 2" lengths.
1 - 2 carrots Cut in halves lengthwise, then slant cut.
2 scallions Slant-cut.
½ - 1 teaspoon oil
1½ tablespoons Chinese fermented black beans Rinse and drain.
1 tablespoon minced garlic or to taste
1 - 2 tablespoons minced shallots
1 teaspoon grated fresh ginger or to taste
¼ - 1 teaspoon Asian chili sauce or to taste (optional)
½ - 1 cup pork or chicken broth
kosher salt to taste

❀ In a wok or large frying pan, bring 2 tablespoons broth to a boil, using high heat. Add napa cabbage, carrots and scallions. Stir fry till vegetables are slightly under desired doneness, about 5 minutes for crisp-tender. Remove vegetables and any broth to a platter.

❀ Add oil to wok. Add fermented black beans, garlic, shallots, ginger and chili sauce. Stir-fry over medium heat till fragrant. Add ¼ cup broth, bring to boil.

❀ Turn heat to high. Add pork. Stir-fry till pork is cooked, adding more broth as needed for gravy. Stir in vegetables. Salt to taste. Serve.

Serves 4 - 5

Variations on the Theme

Pork & Chinese Long Beans with Fermented Black Beans

Substitute: *¾ - 1 pound Chinese long beans* for the *napa cabbage*.
　　　　　Remove ends from beans. Cut beans into about 1½" lengths.
❀　Stir fry till crisp-tender, about 4 - 5 minutes.

Veal & Green Beans with Fermented Black Beans

Substitute: *1 pound boneless veal* for the *pork*
　　　　　¾ - 1 pound green beans for the *napa cabbage*.
　　　　　Remove ends and string beans. Leave whole or cut into
　　　　　shorter lengths.
❀　Stir-fry till slightly under desired doneness.

Veal & Swiss Chard with Fermented Black Beans

Substitute: *1 pound boneless veal* for the *pork*
　　　　　1 pound Swiss chard stems (see note) for the *napa cabbage*.
　　　　　Peel Swiss chard stems. Slant cut into about ½" pieces.
Add: *5 - 8 Chinese dried mushrooms*.
　　　Soak mushrooms in warm water at least 30 minutes to soften.
　　　Discard stems, if any. Shred caps.
❀　Simmer mushrooms in broth for 3 - 5 minutes before adding
Swiss chard and carrots.

NOTE: Save Swiss chard leaves for another use. Cook as you would cook spinach or stir-fry with minced garlic in olive oil.

Pork in Chili Garlic Sauce

1 pound lean boneless pork loin Remove and discard all visible fat. Slice thinly (about 2"× ½"×⅛").

1 teaspoon sugar *2 teaspoons regular soy sauce* *2 teaspoons dark soy sauce* *½ teaspoon kosher salt or to taste* *1 tablespoon cornstarch* *2 tablespoons ginger wine, p.13*	Combine. Add pork. Mix well. Marinate ½ hour at room temperature or overnight in the refrigerator.

1 tablespoon dried cloud ears Soak in warm water ½ hour to soften. Wash well in several changes of water to remove any sand and grit. Break into smaller pieces if desired.

*1 8-ounce can sliced water chestnut*s

1 bunch scallions Cut into 1½" lengths.

1 fresh red chili pepper If available, cut into thin rings.

1 head garlic Peel and slice thinly or mince.

1 - 3 teaspoons Asian chili sauce or to taste

1 - 2 teaspoons oil

½ - 1 cup chicken or pork broth

½ cup coarsely chopped Chinese parsley (optional)

kosher salt to taste

❀   Heat wok. Add oil and garlic. Stir-fry over medium heat till garlic is translucent. Add cloud ears, chili sauce and ¼ cup broth. Bring to a boil, using high heat. Add pork. Stir-fry till pork changes color, 3 - 5 minutes, adding broth as needed to prevent burning.

❀   Add water chestnuts, scallions and fresh chili. Stir-fry till pork is cooked and water chestnuts are heated through, another 3 - 5 minutes, adding broth as needed for gravy. Add salt to taste. Transfer to serving platter. Sprinkle Chinese parsley on top. Serve.

Serves 4 - 6

VARIATIONS ON THE THEME

PORK & BROCCOLI IN CHILI GARLIC SAUCE

Substitute: *¼ cup bamboo shoots* for the *water chestnuts.*
Use only: *1 - 2 scallions.*
Add: *a few carrot slices* for color
    1 pound broccoli Cut florets into bite-sized pieces. Peel and cut
    stems into bite-sized pieces. Put all broccoli in a large container.
    Cover with boiling water. Stir. Drain. Cool under cold running
    water. Drain well.

❁   Add about ¼ cup broth and ½ teaspoon salt to wok. Bring to a boil,
using high heat. Add blanched broccoli to wok. Stir-fry till slightly
under desired doneness, 3 - 5 minutes for crisp-tender. Add more broth,
1 tablespoon at a time, as needed, to prevent burning. Remove broccoli
and any broth to a platter.

❁   Continue with recipe at left.

VEAL & ASPARAGUS IN CHILI GARLIC SAUCE

Substitute: *1 pound boneless veal* for the *pork*
          1 pound asparagus for the *broccoli.*
          Peel asparagus (see p.26) if needed. Remove scales. Cut
          into about 1½" lengths.

VEAL & MIXED VEGETABLES IN CHILI GARLIC SAUCE

Substitute: *1 pound boneless veal* for the *pork*
          ½ - 1 cup each of sliced celery, sliced carrots, sliced
          bamboo shoots, sliced bok choy or *other vegetable* for the
          broccoli.

PORK WITH THREE PEPPERS

1 pound lean boneless pork loin chops Remove and discard all visible fat. Cut into about ⅛" thick slices.

¼ teaspoon Asian chili sauce or to taste
½ teaspoon sugar
1 tablespoon cornstarch
2 tablespoons ginger wine, p.13
1 - 2 tablespoons hoisin sauce or to taste
1 tablespoon regular soy sauce

Combine. Add pork. Mix well. Marinate ½ hour at room temperature or overnight in the refrigerator.

1 medium red pepper
1 medium yellow pepper
1 medium green pepper

Remove and discard seeds and membranes. Cut into strips the same size as the pork.

1 teaspoon minced garlic
½ teaspoon oil
½ teaspoon sesame oil (optional)
1 tablespoon Chinkiang vinegar
½ - 1 cup pork or chicken broth
kosher salt to taste

❀   In a wok or large frying pan, bring 2 tablespoons broth to a boil, using high heat. Add peppers. Stir-fry till peppers are just heated through, about 2 - 3 minutes. Remove peppers and any remaining broth to a platter.

❀   Add ½ teaspoon oil and garlic to wok. Stir-fry till lightly browned, using medium heat. Add ½ cup broth. Bring to a boil, using high heat. Add pork and stir-fry till just cooked, about 5 minutes. Stir in peppers, vinegar, sesame oil and additional broth as needed for gravy. Add salt to taste. Serve.

Serves 4 - 6

Variations on the Theme

Pork with Chinese Eggplant

Substitute: *3 - 4 Chinese eggplants* for the *peppers*.
Remove and discard eggplant caps. Cut in halves lengthwise, then slant-cut into about ¼" thick pieces.

❀ Stir-fry eggplant until tender, about 3 - 5 minutes.

Add: *1 small onion*. Coarsely chop. Add to wok at the same time as
garlic.

Veal with Jicama

Substitute: *1 pound boneless veal* for the *pork*.
Use only: *⅓ of red, yellow and green peppers*.
Add: *1 - 2 cups sliced jicama* (slices about fingersize and ⅛" thick).

Veal with Fresh Shiitake Mushrooms

Substitute: *1 pound boneless veal* for the *pork*.
Use only: *a few strips of red, green and yellow peppers*.
Add: *8 ounces fresh shiitake mushrooms*.
Remove stems, cut into very thin slices. Cut caps into ½" wide
strips.

Veal with Mixed Vegetables

Substitute: *1 pound boneless veal* for the *pork*.
Use only: *a few strips of red, green and yellow peppers*.
Add: *2 - 3 ounces fresh mushrooms* Cut into ¼" thick slices.
1 small onion Cut into 6 or 8 wedges.
3 - 4 stalks asparagus Peel and cut into 1" lengths.
1 rib celery Slant-cut into about ¼" thick slices.

Or use any combination of vegetables on hand.

PORK WITH CHINESE CHIVES

1 pound lean boneless pork loin Remove and discard all visible fat.
   Shred.

1 tablespoon cornstarch
1 tablespoon ginger wine, p.13
2 tablespoons hoisin sauce
1 tablespoon regular soy sauce
1 teaspoon sugar or to taste

Combine. Add pork. Mix well.
Marinate ½ hour at room temperature or overnight in the
refrigerator.

1 tablespoon cloud ears Soak in warm water ½ hour to soften.
   Wash well in several changes of water to remove any sand and
   grit. Break into smaller pieces, if desired.
4 - 6 ounces Chinese chives or scallion Cut into about 1½" lengths.
1 8-ounce can shredded bamboo shoots Drain. Rinse. Cut into
   shorter lengths, if desired.
shredded carrot or red pepper for color
¼ - 1 teaspoon minced garlic
½ teaspoon oil
½ - 1 cup pork or chicken broth
kosher salt to taste

❀   In a wok or large frying pan, over high heat, bring ¼ cup broth
to a boil. Add cloud ears, chives, bamboo shoots and carrots. Stir-fry
till carrots are slightly under desired doneness, about 3 - 5 minutes
for crisp tender. Remove vegetables and any broth to a platter.

❀   Add oil and garlic to wok. Stir-fry till garlic is lightly browned.
Add ¼ cup broth, bring to a boil, using high heat. Add pork. Stir-fry
till pork is cooked, another 4 - 5 minutes, adding more broth as
needed. Mix in vegetables. Add salt to taste.

❀   Serve with rice, steamed Chinese pancakes or steamed pita. If
serving with Chinese pancakes or pita, the dish should not have a lot
of gravy.

Serves 4 - 6

Serving suggestions

With Chinese Pancakes

Place the following condiments in individual small dishes for diners to choose from when making pancake rolls.

hoisin sauce, Asian chili sauce or Asian chili oil, finely shredded lettuce, coarsely chopped unsalted roasted peanuts, coarsely chopped Chinese parsley.

10 - 15 Chinese pancakes, homemade or store-bought.

❀   Place stacked Chinese pancakes on a damp steamer cloth or cheesecloth. Steam (see p.186) on high heat, 7 - 10 minutes or till pliable. To assemble, see page 46.

With pita

Condiments as above except substitute *whole Boston lettuce leaves* for the *finely shredded lettuce.*

8 - 12 small pitas Cut each pita into 2 half-moons.

❀   Place sliced pita on a damp steamer cloth or cheesecloth. Steam (see p.186) on high heat, 5 - 7 minutes or till pliable.

TO SERVE: Brush a bit of hoisin sauce on the inside of a steamed pita. Place a piece of lettuce inside, leaving the leaf edge extending past the edge of the pita. Fill with 1 - 2 tablespoons of cooked Pork with Chinese Chives. Top with condiments of choice. Enjoy.

Variation on the theme

Pork with Spaghetti Squash

Substitute: *1 pound spaghetti squash* for the *bamboo shoots.*

❀   Remove and discard seeds from spaghetti squash. Cut into 2 or 3 large chunks. Put into a pot with about ½" of water. Cover and cook 10 - 15 minutes. The squash should still have some crunch to it. Cool under cold running water. Drain. Separate into strands, using a fork.

PORK WITH CHINESE CHIVES (continued)

Assembling Pork with Chinese Chives & Chinese Pancakes

1. Place a steamed pancake on a plate. Brush a thin layer of hoisin sauce down the center of pancake.

2. Place 1-2 tablespoons lettuce on top of hoisin sauce, about two-thirds the lengths of the pancake. Top with 2 tablespoons of pork mixture and condiments of your choice.

3. Fold one side of pancake over filling.

4. Fold end of pancake (without filling) over.

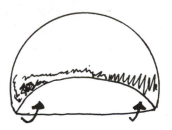

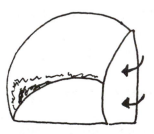

5. Fold other side of pancake over.

6. Pick up wrapped pancake with fingers. Eat, starting at open end.

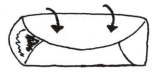

Wokking Your Way to Low Fat Cooking

CURRY PORK

2 pounds lean boneless pork shoulder Remove and discard all visible
fat. Cut into about ½" cubes.
4 plum tomatoes Peel, seed and chop coarsely.
1 pound red skin potatoes Peel and cut into about ½" cubes.
1 large onion Chop coarsely.
2 shallots, minced
2 - 3 cloves garlic, minced
½ - 3 teaspoons Asian chili sauce or to taste
2 - 4 tablespoons curry powder or to taste
1 teaspoon kosher salt or to taste
¼ cup ginger wine, p.13
1 cup pork or chicken broth
1 teaspoon oil

❀   Heat wok. Add oil. Add curry powder. Stir-fry 5 seconds, using
medium heat. Add onion, shallots and garlic. Stir-fry till onion wilts,
about 2 minutes, adding broth 1 tablespoon at a time to prevent
burning.

❀   Add pork, chili sauce and salt. Stir-fry till pork cubes change
color, adding ginger wine 1 tablespoon at a time to prevent burning.

❀   Add tomatoes and potatoes. Mix well. Transfer all to a heavy pot.
Add broth to wok. Swirl to loosen any curry mixture. Pour over pork
in pot. Bring to boil. Cover and simmer about 45 minutes, or till pork
is tender. Serve with lots of rice. Curry Pork tastes better if made the
day before serving.

Serves 7 - 10

VARIATION ON THE THEME

CURRY LAMB

Substitute: *lamb* for the *pork.*

PORK & SZECHUAN PRESERVED VEGETABLES

1 pound lean boneless pork loin Remove and discard all visible fat.
Shred.

½ teaspoon sugar
1 tablespoon cornstarch
2 tablespoons ginger wine, p.13
1 tablespoon regular soy sauce
1 tablespoon dark soy sauce

Combine. Add pork. Mix well.
Marinate 1 hour at room
temperature or overnight in the
refrigerator.

½ - 1 cup shredded Szechuan preserved vegetables Rinse and drain.
1 pound bean sprouts Wash and drain well.
1 cup shredded red pepper
¾ - 1 cup 1" lengths of Chinese chives or scallion
3 - 4 Chinese dried mushrooms Soak in warm water at least ½ hour
to soften. Remove and discard any stems. Shred caps.
1 teaspoon minced garlic or to taste
½ - 1 teaspoon oil
½ cup pork or chicken broth
8 small pitas Cut each pita in half (crosswise into half moons)
hoisin sauce (optional) To brush on pita.

❀   Add water to steamer base. Line steamer basket or steamer rack
with a damp clean towel or cheesecloth. Bring water to boil. Arrange
pita halves on top of steamer cloth, overlapping if necessary. Steam
(see p.186) covered, for about 7 minutes or till pliable.

❀   In a wok or large frying pan, bring 2 tablespoons broth to a boil
using medium heat. Add Szechuan preserved vegetables. Boil 1
minute.

❀   Turn heat to high. Add bean sprouts, red pepper and chives.
Cook till bean sprouts have lost their rawness, 2-3 minutes. Remove
vegetables and any remaining broth to a platter.

❀   Add oil, garlic and mushroom to wok. Stir-fry using medium-

PORK & SZECHUAN PRESERVED VEGETABLES (cont.)

heat till fragrant. Add remaining broth. Bring to a boil, using high heat. Add pork. Stir-fry till pork is just cooked. Stir in vegetables. Serve.

Serves 4 - 6

SERVING SUGGESTIONS

TO SERVE: Brush a bit of hoisin sauce on the inside of a steamed pita. Fill pita with pork mixture and enjoy.

VARIATIONS ON THE THEME

Substitute one or a combination of the following for the bean *sprouts: 1 pound shredded napa cabbage*
1 - 2 cups shredded jicama or water chestnuts
1 - 1½ pounds shredded kohlrabi
1 - 1¼ pound shredded daikon

In a hurry? Use *boneless pork loin chops*. Cut into about ⅛" thick slices. Slice (instead of shredding) vegetables. Serve with rice or noodles.

PORK & SZECHUAN PRESERVED VEGETABLES LO MEIN

Substitute: *1 pound fresh Chinese egg noodles* for the *pita.*
❁   Cook egg noodles in boiling water for 7 minutes. Drain. Toss with 1 - 2 tablespoons mushroom soy sauce and 1 teaspoon Asian sesame oil, if desired. Spread on a large serving platter. Spoon cooked Pork & Szechuan Preserved Vegetables over noodles. Toss and serve.

VEAL & SZECHUAN PRESERVED VEGETABLES

Substitute: *1 pound boneless veal* for the *pork.*

PORK WITH SUMMER SQUASH

1 pound lean boneless pork loin chops. Remove and discard all
visible fat. Cut into about ⅛" thick slices.

½ teaspoon brown sugar
1 tablespoon cornstarch
2 tablespoons ginger wine, p.13
1 tablespoon regular soy sauce
1 tablespoon mushroom soy sauce
⎤ Combine. Add pork. Mix
well. Marinate 1 hour at
room temperature or over-
night in the refrigerator.

¾ pound zucchini
¾ pound yellow squash
⎤ Cut in halves lengthwise, then slant-cut
into about ¼" thick slices.

1 carrot Cut in half lengthwise then slant-cut into ⅛" thick slices.
3 - 4 Chinese dried mushrooms Soak in warm water at least ½ hour
to soften. Remove and discard any stems. Cut caps into thin
strips.
1 - 2 scallions. Slant-cut.
½ - 1 cup chicken or pork broth
kosher salt to taste

_____

❀   In wok or large frying pan, bring 2 tablespoons broth to a boil,
using high heat. Add carrot and mushrooms. Stir-fry 2 - 4 minutes.
Add squash. Stir-fry till squash is heated through, about 2 - 3
minutes. Remove to a platter, leaving liquid in wok.

❀   Add ¼ cup broth to wok. Bring to boil using high heat. Add pork.
Stir-fry till pork is just cooked. Stir in cooked vegetables, scallion
and additional broth as needed for gravy. Add salt to taste and serve.

Serves 4 - 6

VARIATIONS ON THE THEME

CHILI LOVERS: Add *Asian chili sauce* or *Asian chili garlic sauce*
to taste at the same time as pork.

Pork with Summer Squash (continued)

Pork with Cabbage

Substitute: *1 - 2 pounds green cabbage* or *Savoy cabbage* for the *zucchini* and *yellow squash*. Cut cabbage into ½" wide strips.

Add: *1 tablespoon teriyaki sauce* at the same time as cabbage.

Pork with Broccoli & Cauliflower

Substitute: *¾ pound broccoli florets* and *¾ pound cauliflower* for the *zucchini* and *yellow squash*.

Cut broccoli florets into bite-sized pieces. Blanch and cool. Cut cauliflower into bite-sized pieces.

Add: *2 - 3 teaspoons oyster sauce* and *chili sauce to taste* at the same time as scallion.

Veal with Kohlrabi

Substitute: *1 pound boneless veal* for the *pork*

1 - 1½ pound kohlrabi for the *zucchini* and *yellow squash*.

Peel kohlrabi. Cut into about ¼" thick finger-sized pieces.

Veal with Bok Choy

Substitute: *1 pound boneless veal* for the *pork*

1 pound bok choy for the *green and yellow squash*.

Slant-cut bok choy into about ½" wide pieces.

Add: *2 - 3 teaspoons hoisin sauce* at the same time as pork.

Veal with Sugar Snap Peas

Substitute: *1 pound boneless veal* for the *pork*

¾ - 1 pound sugar snap peas or *snow peas* for the *zucchini* and *yellow squash*.

HOISIN PORK CHOPS

5 lean center-cut pork chops, about ½" thick Remove and discard
   all visible fat.

2 tablespoons brown sugar
2 tablespoons hoisin sauce
1 tablespoon mushroom soy sauce
kosher salt or to taste
2 teaspoons bean sauce or miso
¼ cup ginger wine, p.13
¼ teaspoon five-spice powder
3 - 4 cloves garlic Peel and crush.
1 - 2 scallions, crushed

Combine well in a deep dish
that will hold pork chops in
one layer. Add pork chops.
Turn to coat both sides with
marinade. Cover and marinate
overnight in refrigerator.

2 teaspoons rice vinegar
¼ teaspoon sesame oil (optional)
1 tablespoon chopped Chinese parsley (optional)

1 teaspoon cornstarch
2 teaspoons water

Combine in a small dish. Stir before
adding to saucepan.

❀   Pour 1 cup warm water in the broiler pan. Place broiler rack
on top. Brush rack with lemon juice.

❀   Remove pork chops from marinade. Arrange on broiler rack.
Broil on high, in the middle the of oven, for 6 minutes. Turn. Broil
5 - 6 minutes longer.

❀   Pour marinade into a small saucepan. Add ¼ - ½ cup water.
Bring to a boil. Simmer 5 minutes. Thicken with cornstarch mixture
if sauce is too thin. Stir in rice vinegar and sesame oil. Strain into a
sauce dish.

❀   Arrange pork chops on serving platter. Garnish with chopped
Chinese parsley. Serve.

Serves 3 - 5

Variations on the Theme

Grilled Hoisin Veal Chops

Substitute: *veal chops* for the *pork chops*.
❀   Grill 5 minutes on each side or till desired doneness is reached.

Hoisin Pork Kabobs

Substitute: *1 - 1½ pounds pork cubes (¾" cubes)* for the *pork chops*.
Add: *cherry tomatoes*
   10" - 12" bamboo skewers. Soak in water at least 30 minutes to
   prevent burning.
❀   Thread pork cubes onto bamboo skewers, leaving about 1" free of
meat at the tip. For even cooking leave about ⅛" space between each
cube. Broil or grill 10 - 12 minutes, or till done, turning occasionally.
Place a cherry tomato at the tip of each skewer. Serve.

Hoisin Beef Kabobs

Substitute: *1 - 1½ pound sirloin steak* for the *pork chops*.
         Cut sirloin steak, across the grain, into ¼" thick strips.
Add: *cherry tomatoes*
   10" - 12" bamboo skewers. Soak in water at least 30 minutes to
   prevent burning.
❀   Thread beef strips, accordion-style, onto bamboo skewers, leaving
about 1" free of meat at the tip. Broil or grill 6 - 10 minutes, or till
done, turning occasionally. Place a cherry tomato at the tip of each
skewer. Serve.

PORK CHOPS IN CHINESE RED VINEGAR SAUCE

1 pound lean boneless pork loin Remove and discard all visible fat.
   Cut into about ¼" thick chops.

1 egg, lightly beaten
2 tablespoons ginger wine, p.13
1 tablespoon regular soy sauce
1 tablespoon oyster sauce
1 teaspoon sugar
white pepper to taste

Combine. Add pork chops. Mix well. Marinate overnight in the refrigerator.

2 cups crispy rice cereal, crushed
¼ cup chopped Chinese parsley

Combine in a flat dish or on a sheet of wax paper.

1 teaspoon kosher salt
¼ cup Chinese red vinegar or to taste
2 tablespoons sugar or to taste
2 tablespoons regular soy sauce
2 tablespoons ketchup
¾ - 1 cup water

Combine in a small saucepan. This is the red vinegar sauce.

1 tablespoon cornstarch
2 tablespoons water

Combine in a small dish. Stir well before adding to saucepan.

Chinese parsley for garnish

❀ Coat each pork chop with crispy rice mixture. Place on a baking pan brushed with lemon juice or a non-stick baking pan. Bake at 425°F for 12 - 15 minutes or till just done. Do not overcook.

❀ Bring sauce to boil. Thicken with cornstarch mixture. Spoon a layer of sauce on a serving platter. Arrange pork chops attractively on top of sauce. Garnish with Chinese parsley. Pour remaining sauce into a sauce dish. Serve.

Serves 4 - 5

Variations on the Theme

Turkey Cutlets in Chinese Red Vinegar Sauce

Substitute: *1 pound turkey breast slices* for the *pork chops.*

Lamb Chops in Chinese Red Vinegar Sauce

Substitute: *1 pound lamb chops* for the *pork chops.*

Red Vinegar Noodle Salad

1 pound fresh Chinese egg noodles (see note)
2 - 3 cups bite-sized blanched broccoli florets
2 yellow tomatoes Remove and discard seeds. Cut into thin strips.
½ cup thinly sliced red radish
1 scallion, thinly sliced
¼ cup coarsely chopped Chinese parsley (optional)
Red vinegar sauce (previous page)

❀   Bring red vinegar sauce to boil. Thicken with cornstarch mixture Cool to room temperature.
❀   Cook noodles in boiling water for 7 minutes. Drain. Cool under cold running water. Drain well.
❀   Toss cooled and drained noodles with red vinegar sauce to taste. Mix in vegetables. Serve at room temperature.

NOTE: Any kind of cooked pasta can be substituted for the egg noodles.

IN A HURRY PORK CHOPS

4 lean center-cut pork chops, about ½" thick Remove and discard
    all visible fat.

2 tablespoons hoisin sauce
1½ tablespoons sugar
1 tablespoon ginger wine, p.13   Combine in a small
1 teaspoon kosher salt or to taste   saucepan.
3 - 4 cloves garlic, crushed and peeled

1 teaspoon cornstarch   Combine in a small dish. Stir before
1 tablespoon water   adding to saucepan.

¼ cup chicken or pork broth or water
Chinese parsley for garnish (optional)

❀   Pour 1 cup warm water in the broiler pan. Brush broiler rack
with lemon juice.

❀   Place pork chops on rack. Broil on high, in the middle of the
oven, for 6 minutes. Brush with hoisin mixture and turn.

❀   Broil on high for another 4 minutes. Brush with hoisin mixture.
Broil an additional 1 - 2 minutes or till pork chops are done. Do not
overcook.

❀   Add ¼ cup broth or water to remaining hoisin mixture in saucepan. Bring to a boil. Thicken with cornstarch mixture, if sauce is
too thin. Spoon over cooked pork chops or serve separately. Garnish
chops with Chinese parsley, if desired.

Serves 4

Beef

59
Tomato Beef

60
Szechuan Beef
Szechuan Beef with Daikon
Szechuan Beef with Turnip
Szechuan Beef with Kohlrabi

62
Beef with Broccoli
Beef with Jicama & Asparagus
Beef with Sunchoke & Zucchini
Beef with Straw Mushrooms
& Napa
Beef with Assorted Vegetables

64
Pineapple Beef Kabobs
Citrus Beef Kabobs
(Pineapple Pork Kabobs)
Sesame Pineapple Beef Kabobs
(Sesame Pineapple Turkey
Kabobs)

66
Chili Beef with
Chinkiang Vinegar

68
Tangerine Beef Balls with
Napa
Beef Balls with Bok Choy
Beef Balls with Fuzzy Melon
Beef Patties with Mushroom Sauce
Meatball Stew
Tangerine Beef Balls on a Stick

72
Star Anise Beef with Daikon
Star Anise Beef with Chayote
Star Anise Beef with Red Radish
Star Anise Beef with Fuzzy Melon
Star Anise Beef with Rutabaga

74
Curry Beef

MONEY-SAVING, TIME-SAVING TIPS

Marinating meat in the refrigerator overnight or up to 2 days tenderizes leaner cuts of meat.

Slicing beef across the grain makes it more tender.

A meat mallet is a great tool for tenderizing leaner and less tender cuts of beef.

Some leaner cuts of beef suitable for stir-frying are: bottom round, top round, eye round, round tip, top loin and sirloin.

Freeze at 0° or below.
You can keep: uncooked steaks or roast, up to 1 year
                    uncooked stew meat, up to 4 months
                    uncooked ground beef, up to 3 months
                    cooked beef, up to 3 months.

Make your own ground beef. This way you will know exactly what is in it. You will save money and have a leaner and higher quality product. Grinding your own meat is very easy, especially if you have a food processor.
Remove and discard any visible fat from a piece of lean beef. Cut into 1" cubes. Place in food processor bowl, about ½ pound at a time. Pulse, using the on/off switch, till desired texture is reached.

Tomato Beef

1 pound lean sirloin steak   Remove and discard all visible fat. Cut meat, across the grain, into about ⅛" thick slices.

1 tablespoon cornstarch
2 tablespoons ginger wine, p.13
2 teaspoons brown sugar
1½ teaspoons regular soy sauce
1½ teaspoons dark soy sauce
½ - 1 teaspoon puréed garlic
* or 4 - 5 cloves garlic,* crushed

Combine. Add beef. Mix well. Marinate ½ hour at room temperature or overnight in the refrigerator.

1 small green pepper   Cut into about 1" chunks.
¼ - ½ cup sliced bamboo shoots
1 onion   Cut into about 1" chunks.
4 - 8 plum tomatoes   Blanch. Peel. Cut into quarters, lengthwise. Remove and discard seeds.
½ - 1 cup chicken broth
white pepper to taste
kosher salt to taste
sugar to taste

❀   In wok or frying pan, bring 2 tablespoons broth to a boil, using high heat. Add bamboo shoots and onion. Stir-fry till onion is slightly under desired doneness, 3 - 4 minutes for crisp-tender. Add green peppers. Stir-fry another minute. Remove all vegetables to a platter.

❀   Add about ½ cup broth to wok. Bring to a boil, using high heat. Add beef. Stir-fry till beef is slightly under desired doneness. Add all vegetables. Stir-fry till tomatoes are heated through. Add white pepper, salt and sugar to taste. Serve.

Serves 4 - 6

SZECHUAN BEEF

2 pounds lean stew beef Remove and discard all visible fat. Slice into about ½" thick slices. Blanch in rapidly boiling water for about 1 minute.

2 - 3 whole star anise or to taste
1 stick cinnamon
2 teaspoons Szechuan peppercorn
a thumb-sized piece of ginger, crushed

Tie securely in a loose cheesecloth bag.

2 tablespoons minced garlic or to taste
3 tablespoons chopped onion
1 tablespoon crushed Chinese rock sugar or brown sugar
1 - 4 teaspoons Asian chili sauce or to taste
1 tablespoon bean sauce
3 tablespoons mushroom or dark soy sauce
3 tablespoons regular soy sauce
¼ cup ginger wine, p.13
1 teaspoon oil
2 - 3 cups beef or chicken broth
1 8-ounce can sliced bamboo shoots Rinse and drain.
1 - 2 onions Cut into about 1" chunks.

❀   In a large heavy pot, bring broth to a boil. Add the bag of spices. Let simmer while preparing other ingredients.

❀   Heat wok. Add oil, garlic and chopped onion. Stir-fry, using medium heat, till onion is wilted. Stir in sugar, chili and bean sauce. Turn heat to high. Add beef. Stir-fry till well coated. Add mushroom soy sauce, regular soy sauce and wine. Stir-fry till most of the liquid is absorbed.

❀   Transfer beef and any remaining liquid to pot with broth. Bring to a rolling boil. Lower heat to maintain a slow simmer. Cover and simmer 1 hour. Add bamboo shoots and onion chunks. Bring to a

Szechuan Beef (continued)

boil.   Simmer another 15 minutes or till beef is tender. This dish should have the consistency of a stew. Serve with lots of rice. Szechuan Beef tastes better if made 1 - 2 days before serving.

Serves 6 - 8

Variations on the Theme

Szechuan Beef with Daikon

Substitute: *1 pound daikon* for the *bamboo shoots.*
        Peel daikon. Cut lengthwise into 2 or 4 pieces. Cut each piece into about ½" thick slices.
❀   Simmer daikon for about 30 minutes or till tender.
Add: *1 tablespoon dried cloud ears* at the same time as *bamboo shoots.*
    Soak cloud ears in warm water at least 30 minutes to soften.
    Wash in several changes of water to remove any sand and grit.
    Break into smaller pieces, if desired.
Garnish with: *½ coarsely chopped Chinese parsley,* if desired.

Szechuan Beef with Turnip

Substitute: *½ - 1 pound turnips* for the *bamboo shoots.*
        Peel turnips. Cut into about 1" cubes.
❀   Simmer about 30 minutes or till tender.
Add: *½ - 1 green pepper.* Cut into about 1" squares.
❀   Add at the end. Simmer till heated through or desired doneness reached.

Szechuan Beef with Kohlrabi

Substitute: *1 - 2 kohlrabi* and *1 - 2 carrots* for the *bamboo shoots.*
        Peel kohlrabi and carrots. Cut into about ¼" thick slices.
❀   Add to the pot at the same time as the onion.

BEEF WITH BROCCOLI

1 pound lean sirloin steak Remove and discard all visible fat. Cut
  meat, across the grain, into about ⅛" thick slices.

1 tablespoon cornstarch
1½ tablespoons ginger wine, p.13
few slices ginger from ginger wine   Combine. Add beef. Mix
1 tablespoon oyster sauce   well. Marinate at least ½
2 teaspoons dark soy sauce   hour at room temperature or
¾ teaspoon brown sugar   overnight in the refrigerator.
dash white pepper or to taste

1 bunch broccoli Separate florets. Cut into bite-sized pieces. Peel
  stems. Slant-cut into bite-sized pieces. Place all broccoli into a
  large container. Cover with boiling water. Stir and drain. Cool
  under cold running water. Drain well. Set aside.
1 large onion Peel and cut into 8 - 10 wedges.
1 carrot Peel and cut into thin slices.
1 cup chicken broth
1 teaspoon kosher salt or to taste
1 - 3 cloves garlic, finely minced
¼ - 2 teaspoons Asian chili garlic sauce (optional)
1 - 2 tablespoons thinly sliced or shredded scallion
½ - 1 teaspoon oil

❀   In a wok or large frying pan, bring ¼ cup broth to a boil, using
high heat. Add salt and vegetables. Stir-fry till vegetables are slightly
under desired doneness, 3 - 5 minutes for crisp-tender. Remove
vegetables and drain, reserving any liquid. Spread on a heated platter.

❀   Add oil and garlic to wok. Stir-fry, using medium heat, till garlic
is lightly browned. Add chili garlic sauce, reserved liquid and remaining broth Bring to a boil, using high heat. Add beef. Stir-fry till beef
reaches desired doneness. Ladle on top of vegetables. Garnish with
scallion and serve.

Serves 4 - 5

Variations on the theme

Beef with Jicama & Asparagus

Substitute: *½ pound jicama* and *¾ - 1 pound asparagus* for the
broccoli.
　　　　Peel jicama. Cut into about 2"× ½"×⅛" thick slices.
　　　　Peel asparagus (see p.26). Cut into about 2" lengths.

Beef with Sunchokes & Zucchini

Substitute: *½ - 1 pound sunchokes* and *2 - 3 small zucchini* for the
broccoli.
　　　　Peel sunchokes. Cut into about ¼" thick slices.
　　　　Cut zucchini into about ¼" thick slices.

If you like your sunchoke crisp, no cooking adjustment is required.
If you like your sunchoke tender, cook 2 - 3 minutes before adding
zucchini, onion and carrot.

Beef with Straw Mushrooms & Napa

Substitute: *1 15-ounce can straw mushrooms* and *1 - 2 pounds napa
cabbage* for the *broccoli.*
　　　　Drain and rinse straw mushrooms.
　　　　Cut napa cabbage into 3 or 4 lengthwise strips. Cut strips
　　　　into 2" lengths.

Beef with Assorted Vegetables

Substitute: any available *seasonal vegetables,* alone or in combina-
tions, for the *broccoli.*

PINEAPPLE BEEF KABOBS

1 pound lean boneless beef sirloin steak Remove and discard all
   visible fat. Cut steak into ¾" cubes.

1 tablespoon ginger wine, p.13
3 tablespoons regular soy sauce
2 - 3 tablespoons concentrated
   pineapple juice
1 tablespoon rice vinegar
2 teaspoons brown sugar
white pepper or to taste
kosher salt to taste

Combine in a container large
enough to hold beef. Add beef.
Marinate ½ hour at room temperature, or preferably overnight
in the refrigerator.

1 15-ounce can pineapple chunks Drain. Reserve liquid.
1 - 2 green peppers Cut into 1" squares.
1 - 2 red peppers Cut into 1" squares.

juice from canned pineapple
1 tablespoon regular soy sauce
2 tablespoons ketchup
1 tablespoon cornstarch
¼ cup water

Combine in a small saucepan.
Bring to boil, stirring constantly,
till thickened. Remove from heat.
This is the sauce.

10" - 12" bamboo skewers Soak in water for at least 30 minutes to
   prevent burning.

❀   Thread beef onto bamboo skewers, alternating with pineapple
and green and red peppers.

❀   Brush kabobs with sauce. Broil in the middle of the oven, or
grill, 6 - 10 minutes, or till done, turning occasionally. Serve.

Serves 4 - 6

VARIATIONS ON THE THEME

Add or substitute: *small mushrooms, water chestnuts or other vegetables of choice* for the *green peppers* or *red peppers.*
Add to the marinade: *Asian chili sauce to taste* if you like spicy food.

CITRUS BEEF KABOBS

Substitute: *¼ cup fresh-squeezed orange juice* for the *pineapple juice*
1 tablespoon fresh lime juice and *1 tablespoon fresh lemon juice* for the *rice vinegar.*
Increase sugar to: *1½ tablespoons brown sugar*

PINEAPPLE PORK KABOBS

Substitute: *lean pork sirloin* for the *beef sirloin steak.*

SESAME PINEAPPLE BEEF KABOBS

Add: *1 teaspoon Asian sesame oil* to the marinade
1 - 2 tablespoons toasted sesame seeds.
Eliminate: *green peppers* and *red peppers*
❀ Slice sirloin steak into thin (about ⅛" thick) long strips instead of cubes. Thread marinated beef accordion style onto bamboo skewers. Top skewers with a pineapple chunk. Brush with sauce. Sprinkle on toasted sesame seeds. Broil or grill.

SESAME PINEAPPLE TURKEY KABOBS

Substitute: *turkey breast meat* for the *sirloin steak.*
Slice turkey breast, along the grain, into thin (about ⅛" thick) long strips.

CHILI BEEF WITH CHINKIANG VINEGAR

1 pound lean sirloin steak Remove and discard all visible fat. Cut meat, across the grain, into about ⅛" thick slices.

1 tablespoon cornstarch
1½ tablespoons ginger wine, p.13
1 tablespoon mushroom soy sauce
2 teaspoons regular soy sauce
1 teaspoon brown sugar
½ teaspoon salt or to taste
white pepper to taste

Combine. Add beef. Mix well. Marinate at least ½ hour at room temperature or overnight in the refrigerator.

1- 2 teaspoons minced garlic or to taste
1 - 2 ribs celery Slant cut into about ¼" thick slices.
½ - 1 can (8-ounce) sliced bamboo shoots
1½ tablespoons cloud ears Soak in warm water ½ hour to soften. Wash well in several changes of water to remove any sand and grit. Break into smaller pieces, if desired.
2 - 4 scallions Cut into about 1" lengths.
1 - 3 fresh red chili peppers Cut into thin rings.
1 - 3 teaspoons Asian chili sauce or to taste
1 tablespoon Chinkiang vinegar or to taste
additional brown sugar to taste
additional kosher salt to taste
1 teaspoon oil
½ - 1 cup beef or chicken broth

❀ Heat wok or large frying pan. Add oil and garlic. Stir-fry, using medium heat, till garlic is lightly browned. Add celery, bamboo shoots, cloud ears, scallions and fresh chili peppers. Stir-fry, using high heat, till vegetables are heated through, adding broth 1 tablespoon at a time to prevent burning. Remove to a platter.

❀ Add ¼ cup broth to wok. Bring to a boil, using high heat. Add beef and Asian chili sauce. Stir-fry till beef is nearly cooked, 3 - 5 minutes, adding more broth as needed for gravy. Add vegetables.

CHILI BEEF WITH CHINKIANG VINEGAR (continued)

Stir-fry till beef is cooked, 2 - 3 minutes more. Stir in Chinkiang vinegar. Add sugar and salt to taste. Serve.

Serves 3 - 5

VARIATIONS ON THE THEME

VARIATION 1

Substitute: *1 - 2 onions* for the *celery*
sliced water chestnuts for the *bamboo shoots*
3 - 6 Chinese dried mushrooms for the *cloud ears*
1 cup 1" lengths Chinese chives for the *scallions.*
Cut onions into 6 or 8 wedges.
Soak mushrooms in warm water, at least 30 minutes to soften. Remove and discard any stems. Shred caps.

❀ Add mushrooms to oil at the same time as garlic.

Add: *¼ - ½ cup chopped Chinese parsley.*

❀ Stir in parsley at the same time as the Chinkiang vinegar.

VARIATION 2

Substitute: *1 - 2 pounds napa cabbage* for the *celery, bamboo shoots* and *cloud ears.*
Cut napa lengthwise into ¾" wide strips, cut strips into 1½" lengths.

VARIATION 3

Substitute: *3 - 4 Chinese eggplants* for the *celery, bamboo shoots* and *cloud ears.*
Remove eggplant caps. Cut eggplants in half lengthwise. Slice into ¼" thick slices.

Tangerine Beef Balls with Napa

1 pound ground top round Remove all visible fat before grinding.

a thumb-sized piece of dried tangerine peel or *to taste* Soak in
warm water at least 30 minutes to soften. Scrape away and
discard the softened pith. Mince the remaining peel.
¼ cup finely chopped Chinese parsley
¼ cup finely chopped carrots
1 - 2 scallions, finely chopped

1 egg, lightly beaten
1 teaspoon kosher salt or to taste
1 teaspoon brown sugar
1 tablespoon cornstarch
1 tablespoon regular soy sauce
1 tablespoon ginger wine. p.13
dash of white pepper or to taste
½ teaspoon Asian sesame oil (optional)

Combine with beef,
tangerine peel, parsley,
carrots, and scallion. Mix
well. Can be done the day
before and refrigerated.

1 - 2 pounds napa cabbage Cut into 1" pieces.
½ - 1 cup asparagus pieces for color
a few slices of carrot for color (optional)
1 1.7 or 2-ounce bag bean thread Soak at least 15 minutes in warm
water to soften. Cut into 2 - 3" lengths.
1 tablespoon oyster sauce (optional)
1 scallion, thinly sliced
1 - 1½ cups beef or chicken broth
kosher salt to taste

❀   Form beef mixture into walnut-sized meatballs. Place on baking
pan brushed with lemon juice or a non-stick baking pan. Bake
uncovered at 350ºF for 25 - 30 minutes.

❀   Place napa cabbage in a wok or Dutch oven. Add meatballs
and 1 cup broth. Bring to a boil. Cover and simmer till napa is soft,
30 - 45 minutes. Add asparagus, carrot slices and bean thread. Cook

TANGERINE BEEF BALLS WITH NAPA (continued)

another 2 - 3 minutes, adding more broth as needed for gravy. Stir in oyster sauce and scallion. Add salt to taste. Serve.

Serves 4 - 6

NOTE: These meatballs freeze well. Make extra for the freezer.

VARIATIONS ON THE THEME

BEEF BALLS WITH BOK CHOY

Substitute: *1 - 2 pounds bok choy* for the *napa*.
        Slant-cut bok choy into about ½" thick slices.
Add: *¼ - 2 teaspoons Asian chili sauce or to taste*
    1 tablespoon cornstarch combined with 2 tablespoons water.
Eliminate: *bean thread*.
❀   Place meatballs and ¾ cup broth in a wok or Dutch oven. Bring to a boil, using high heat. Cover and simmer 5 - 10 minutes. Stir in bok choy; return to a boil, using high heat. Cook till bok choy reaches desired doneness, about 3 - 5 minutes for crisp-tender bok choy. Stir in oyster sauce and chili sauce. Add salt to taste. Thicken with cornstarch mixture, as needed. Serve.

BEEF BALLS WITH FUZZY MELON

Substitute: *1½ - 2 pounds fuzzy melon* for the *napa*.
        Peel fuzzy melon. Cut into ½" thick slices or 1" cubes.
❀   Place meatballs and fuzzy melon in a large pot. Add 1 cup broth. Bring to a boil. Cover and simmer till fuzzy melon is tender, 35 - 45 minutes or till reached desired doneness. Add bean thread and carrot slices. Cook another 2 - 3 minutes. Stir in oyster sauce and scallion. Add salt to taste. Serve.

BEEF PATTIES WITH MUSHROOM SAUCE

Add: *1 - 2 teaspoons oyster sauce* to meat mixture
   1 tablespoon fresh tangerine juice or *fresh orange juice* or
   broth or *water* to meat mixture.

❀   Form meat mixture into 4 patties (about ¾" thick). Place on
a baking pan brushed with lemon juice or a non-stick pan. Broil,
on high, in the middle of the oven, for 7 minutes. Turn. Broil
another 7 - 10 minutes, or till cooked. Place on a serving platter.
Spoon mushroom sauce (recipe below) over patties. Garnish
with some fresh parsley. Serve.

MUSHROOM SAUCE

3 - 4 Chinese dried mushrooms Soak at least 30 minutes in warm
   water to soften. Remove and discard any stems. Finely chop
   caps.
4 ounces fresh mushrooms, coarsely chopped
1 - 2 scallions Cut into thin rings or slant-cut.
2 teaspoons mushroom soy sauce
kosher salt to taste
white pepper to taste
¾ cup chicken broth
1 teaspoon oil

1½ teaspoons cornstarch⎤ Combine in a small dish. Stir well
1 tablespoon water   ⎦ before adding to wok.

———————————————

❀   Heat wok. Add oil and Chinese mushrooms. Stir-fry, using
medium heat, till mushrooms are fragrant, 2 - 3 minutes. Add fresh
mushrooms, stir-fry 2 - 3 minutes longer, adding broth 1 tablespoon
at a time if wok is dry. Stir in mushroom soy sauce and white pepper. Add remaining broth. Bring to a boil. Simmer 3 minutes longer.
Thicken with cornstarch mixture.
NOTE: Try serving beef patties on a bun with a slice of sweet onion,
lettuce, tomato, and ketchup for Chinese-American hamburgers.

TANGERINE BEEF BALLS WITH NAPA (continued)

MEATBALL STEW

Eliminate: *napa cabbage* and *bean thread.*
Add: *1 - 3 carrots* Peel and cut into about ½" thick pieces.
   1 - 2 chayote Peel. Discard seeds. Cut into about 1" cubes.
   4 - 6 ounces small mushrooms
   1 - 2 onions Cut into about 1" chunks.
   1 or more potatoes Cut into about 1" chunks.
   1 or more dried or fresh chili peppers (optional)
   ¼ cup or more coarsely chopped Chinese parsley (optional)
❀   Place meatballs, carrots, chayote, mushrooms, onions, potatoes
and chili peppers in a large pot. Add broth to barely cover. Bring to
a boil. Cover and simmer till vegetables are tender, about 30 minutes.
Stir in Chinese parsley, oyster sauce and salt to taste. Thicken with
cornstarch and water mixture, if needed.

TANGERINE BEEF BALLS ON A STICK

Add: *1 can pineapple chunks* Drain and reserve liquid.
   8" - 10" bamboo skewers Soak in water for 30 minutes to prevent
   burning.
❀   Thread meatballs on bamboo skewers alternating with pineapple
chunks. Brush with reserved pineapple liquid. Broil 3 - 4 minutes, or
till heated through.

I have attempted to give you some ideas of ways to serve this versatile
ground beef mixture. I am sure you will be able to come up with your
own creative ideas. If you would like to share your favorite recipes, I
would love to hear from you.

STAR ANISE BEEF WITH DAIKON

2 pounds lean stew beef Remove and discard all visible fat. Cut into 1" cubes.

1½ tablespoon ginger wine, p.13
3 tablespoons dark soy sauce
1 square red bean curd, mashed (about 1 tablespoon)
1 tablespoon crushed Chinese rock sugar (or brown sugar)
½ teaspoon five-spice powder

Combine. Marinate overnight in the refrigerator.

2 - 3 pounds daikon Peel and cut into about 1¼" cubes.
6 - 12 slices ginger from ginger wine
½ cup sliced scallions
2 - 4 cloves garlic, minced
1 teaspoon oil
kosher salt to taste
2 - 3 whole star anise or to taste
3 - 4 cups beef or chicken broth

2 - 3 tablespoons cornstarch
¼ cup water or broth

Combine. Stir well before adding to pot.

❀   Add broth and star anise to a pot large enough to hold broth, beef and daikon. Bring to a boil. Let simmer while preparing other ingredients.

❀   Heat wok. Add oil, ginger, scallions and garlic. Stir-fry over medium heat till scallions wilt. Turn heat to high. Add beef. Stir-fry till color changes. Transfer to pot with broth. Bring to a boil. Lower heat to maintain a slow simmer. Simmer 1 hour.

❀   Add daikon to beef. Return to a boil. Lower heat and simmer an additional 45 - 60 minutes. Thicken with cornstarch mixture. Serve.

Serves 6 - 8

VARIATIONS ON THE THEME

STAR ANISE BEEF WITH CHAYOTE

Substitute: *3 - 5 chayote* for the *daikon*
> Peel chayote. Cut in half lengthwise. Remove and discard seeds. Cut into about 1¼" cubes.

Add: *¼ - ½ cup coarsely chopped Chinese parsley.*

❀ Stir in Chinese parsley after thickening with cornstarch mixture.

STAR ANISE BEEF WITH RED RADISH

Substitute: *1 pound large peeled red radishes* for the *daikon.*
Add: *1 pound carrots*
> *1 - 2 onions.*
> Peel and cut carrots and onions into about 1" chunks.

STAR ANISE BEEF WITH FUZZY MELON

Substitute: *2 - 3 pounds fuzzy melon* for the *daikon.*
> Peel fuzzy melon. Cut into about 1½ " cubes.

Add: *¼ cup thinly sliced scallions.*

❀ Remove beef and fuzzy melon to serving platter. Sprinkle sliced scallions on top and serve.

STAR ANISE BEEF WITH RUTABAGA

Substitute: *2 - 3 pounds rutabaga* for the *daikon.*
> Peel rutabaga. Cut into about 1" cubes.

Add: *1 stick cinnamon*
> *6 - 8 peppercorns.*

❀ Add cinnamon and peppercorns at the same time as star anise.

CURRY BEEF

1 pound lean sirloin steak. Remove and discard all visible fat. Cut
   meat across the grain into about ⅛" thick strips.

1½ tablespoons cornstarch
1 tablespoon ginger wine, p.13   Combine. Add beef. Mix well.
1 teaspoon sugar   Marinate at least ½ hour at room
2 teaspoons regular soy sauce   temperature or overnight in the
1 teaspoon dark soy sauce   refrigerator.
½ teaspoon salt or to taste

1 teaspoon oil
1 - 3 tablespoons curry powder or to taste
¼ - 2 teaspoons Asian chili sauce or to taste
1 tablespoon minced garlic or to taste
1 pound onions   Cut into lengthwise strips.
1½ - 2 cups beef or chicken broth

_____

❋   Heat wok. Add oil and curry powder. Stir-fry over medium heat
for 10 seconds. Add chili sauce and garlic. Stir-fry till garlic is soft,
adding broth a tablespoon at a time if wok is dry.

❋   Turn heat to high. Add onion and broth as needed. Stir-fry till
onion is translucent.

❋   Add remaining broth. Bring to a boil. Add beef. Stir-fry till beef
is cooked, adding more broth if needed. This is a somewhat soupy
dish. Serve with lots of rice. Curry Beef tastes better if made 1 - 2
days before serving.

Serves 4 - 5

SEAFOOD

77
Bay Scallops with
Green Peas

78
Sea Scallops & Broccoli
Sea Scallops & Tomatoes
Sea Scallops &
Mixed Vegetables

80
Stir-Fry Fish Fillets
Stir-fry Fish Fillets & Asparagus
Stir-fry Fish Fillets &
Vidalia Onions

82
Sweet & Sour Fish

83
Stir-fry Salmon with
Fermented Black Beans

84
Steamed Salmon with
Fermented Black Beans
Steamed Whole Sea Bass with
Fermented Black Beans

85
Broiled Salmon with
Ginger & Scallions

86
Chili Shrimp with Snow Peas
& Baby Corn

87
Curry Shrimp
Curry Fish

88
Rock Shrimp with Broccoli
Rock Shrimp with Asparagus

MONEY-SAVING, TIME-SAVING TIPS

FISH: Whole fish should have full eyes that are clear and bright and gills that are bright red. Avoid fish with eyes that are sunken and cloudy and/or gills that are gray, green or brown.
Steaks and fillets should have a moist, firm texture and a fresh clean smell. Avoid fish that looks dry and smells fishy.
When stir-frying fish, be gentle and patient. Spread out pieces of fish and allow them to cook undisturbed till their edges begin to turn white. At that point, turn gently to cook the other side.

SHRIMP: "Fresh shrimp" sold in supermarkets and fish markets are actually thawed frozen shrimp. If buying for the freezer, ask for still-frozen shrimp. DO NOT refreeze thawed shrimp. It is now possible to purchase individual quick-frozen shrimp in 4 or 5 pound bags. Stock up when the price is right.
The many species of shrimp now available include white, gray, black, pink, tiger and more.

SCALLOPS: The scallops in supermarkets and fish markets may be thawed frozen scallops. Ask if you are buying for the freezer. DO NOT refreeze thawed scallops. It is now also possible to purchase individual quick-frozen bay and sea scallops. Scallop meat can be creamy white or creamy pink.

If possible, purchase seafood on the day you plan to use it. Rinse under cold running water, pat dry and keep refrigerated til ready to use.

DO NOT overcook seafood. Overcooked fish is dry; overcooked shrimp is tough.

BAY SCALLOPS WITH GREEN PEAS

1 pound bay scallops Wash and drain well.

1 tablespoon cornstarch Gently combine well.
1 tablespoon ginger wine, p.13 Marinate ½ hour if
a few slices ginger from ginger wine time permits (not an
1 tablespoon oyster sauce essential step). This
¼ teaspoon kosher salt can be done the day
½ teaspoon sugar before.
white pepper or to taste

1 - 2 cups frozen green peas Thaw and drain.
kosher salt to taste
¾ cup broth

❋ In a wok or large frying pan, bring broth to a boil, using high heat. Add scallops. Stir-fry till scallops begin to change color. Stir in green peas. Stir-fry till scallops are cooked and peas are heated through. Add salt to taste. Serve.

Serves 3 - 5

VARIATION ON THE THEME

CHILI LOVERS: Add *Asian chili sauce* or *Asian chili oil* to taste any time during cooking.

☺ This has got to be the easiest recipe—less than 10 minutes from start to finish and absolutely no cutting. Who says Chinese cooking is labor intensive? Serve this dish over rice or pasta. What could be more simple?

Sea Scallops & Broccoli

1 pound sea scallops Rinse and pat dry well. Cut each scallop into
  2 or 3 circles of even thickness.

1 tablespoon ginger wine, p.13
a few slices fresh ginger Combine. Add scallops.
2 teaspoons cornstarch Gently toss to coat well.
¼ teaspoon kosher salt or to taste Marinate ½ hour.
dash of white pepper or to taste

1 bunch broccoli Cut florets into bite-sized pieces. Peel stems and
  cut into bite-sized pieces. Place florets and stems into a large
  container. Pour boiling water to cover. Stir and drain at once.
  Cool under cold running water. Drain well.
1 - 2 carrots Peel and slice or slant-cut thinly.
1 onion Cut into 6 or more wedges.
1 teaspoon kosher salt or to taste
½ teaspoon sugar
½ - 1 cup broth
1 tablespoon oyster sauce

2 teaspoons cornstarch Combine in a small dish. Stir well
1 tablespoon water before adding to wok.

❀ In a wok or large frying pan, bring ¼ cup broth to a boil, using
high heat. Add salt, sugar and vegetables. Stir-fry till broccoli is
slightly under desired doneness, 3 - 5 minutes for crisp-tender. Remove all vegetables to platter, leaving liquid in wok.

❀ Add ¼ cup more broth to wok. Bring to a boil, using high heat.
Add scallops. Gently stir-fry till scallops turn white, adding more
broth as needed for gravy. Stir in oyster sauce. Thicken with cornstarch mixture. Stir in vegetables. Serve.

Serves 4 - 5

VARIATIONS ON THE THEME

Add: *1 teaspoon minced garlic or to taste*
    ¼ - 2 teaspoons Asian chili sauce or to taste
    ½ - 1 teaspoon oil.

❁   Remove the liquid from wok at the same time as the vegetables.

❁   Add oil and minced garlic to wok. Stir-fry, using medium heat, till garlic is lightly browned. Add Asian chili sauce and ¼ cup broth. Bring to a boil, using high heat. Add scallops. Gently stir-fry till scallops turn to white, adding more broth as needed for gravy. Stir in oyster sauce. Thicken with cornstarch mixture. Stir in vegetables. Serve.

SEA SCALLOPS & TOMATOES

Substitute: *2 - 4 each red* and *yellow tomatoes* for the *broccoli* and
             carrots.
             Peel tomatoes. Remove and discard seeds. Cut into bite-sized chunks.

Add: *¼ - ½ cup coarsely chopped Chinese parsley.*

❁   Skip the first step on page 78 and go directly to the second step. Add tomatoes at the same time as oyster sauce. Bring to a boil. Thicken with cornstarch mixture. Stir in Chinese parsley. Serve at once.

SEA SCALLOPS & MIXED VEGETABLES

Substitute: *any combination of vegetables* for the *broccoli.*
See pages: 27, 43 & 63 for additional vegetable ideas.

STIR-FRY FISH FILLETS

1 pound fish fillets Cut into bite-sized pieces. ⎤
1 tablespoon cornstarch   Combine well.
1½ - 2 teaspoons ginger juice, p.13 (see note)   Marinate 1 hour
1 tablespoon regular soy sauce   in the refrigerator.
¾ teaspoon kosher salt or to taste   This can be done
½ teaspoon sugar   the day before.
white pepper to taste ⎦

1 - 2 cups bite-sized cauliflower
1 cup carrot slices
1 - 2 cups yellow squash slices
1 medium onion Cut into 6 or more wedges.
2 - 4 ounces sugar snap peas or snow peas
1 tablespoon oyster sauce (optional)
1 - 2 tablespoons thinly sliced or shredded scallion
Kosher salt to taste
½ - 1 cup fish or chicken broth

❀   In a wok or large frying pan, bring ½ cup broth to a boil, using high heat. Add cauliflower and carrots; cook about 1 minute. Add squash, onion and sugar snap peas. Stir-fry till vegetables reach desired doneness, 2 - 3 minutes for crisp-tender. Add salt to taste. Remove all vegetables and spread on a heated platter, draining off and leaving in wok as much liquid as possible.

❀   Return liquid in wok to a boil. Add fish. Gently stir-fry till fish just begins to flake, adding more broth as needed for gravy. Gently stir in oyster sauce. Spoon fish and gravy over vegetables. Garnish with scallion. Serve.

Serves 3 - 4

NOTE: 1 tablespoon ginger wine, p.13, may be substituted for the ginger juice.

STIR-FRY FISH FILLETS (continued)

Most any kind of fish fillet can be used for stir-frying. However, for best results, choose firm, mild-flavored fish.

Fish suitable for stir-frying include: *fillets of pike, trout, catfish, sea bass, flounder, red snapper, perch, or salmon.*

Do not limit yourself to the vegetables given in the recipe. Substitute seasonal vegetables, using one vegetable or a combination to suit your individual or family needs and tastes.

VARIATIONS ON THE THEME

Add: *1 teaspoon minced garlic or to taste*
    2 - 3 teaspoons minced shallots
    ¼ - 1 teaspoon Asian chili oil or Asian chili sauce (optional)
    1 teaspoon oil

✿   Heat wok. Add oil, garlic and shallots. Stir-fry, using medium heat, till garlic is lightly browned. Add chili oil and broth. Bring to a boil, using high heat. Add cauliflower and carrots. Continue with recipe.

STIR-FRY FISH FILLETS & ASPARAGUS

Substitute: *1 - 2 pounds asparagus* for the *vegetables*.
    Peel asparagus (see p.26). Remove scales and cut into 1 - 2" lengths.

STIR-FRY FISH FILLETS & VIDALIA ONIONS

Substitute: *1 - 2 Vidalia onions* for the *vegetables*.
    Peel onion. Cut into bite-sized chunks.

SWEET & SOUR FISH

1 pound flounder fillets Leave whole or cut into smaller pieces.

1 tablespoon cornstarch
1 tablespoon ginger wine, p.13
¾ teaspoon kosher salt or to taste
1 teaspoon regular soy sauce

Combine. Add fish. Mix to coat each piece well. Marinate about 1 hour in the refrigerator.

3 - 5 dried Chinese mushrooms Soak in warm water about ½ hour to soften. Remove and discard any stems. Slice caps thinly.
½ - 1 carrot, shredded
½ - 1 medium onion, sliced thinly
½ - 1 green pepper, sliced thinly
1 cup fish broth, chicken broth or water

1 teaspoon kosher salt or to taste
2 tablespoons sugar
2 tablespoons regular sauce
2 tablespoons ketchup
3 tablespoons vinegar

Combine in a small dish. This is the sweet and sour sauce.

❀ In a wok or large frying pan, bring broth to a boil. Add mushrooms, carrots, onion and green pepper. Cook till desired doneness is reached. Remove and spread on a serving platter, leaving liquid in wok.

❀ Add sweet and sour sauce to wok. Bring to a boil. Add fish. Gently stir-fry till fish is cooked. Arrange cooked fish on top of vegetables. Spoon sauce over fish. Serve.

Serves 3 - 4

VARIATION ON THE THEME

Eliminate: *cornstarch* from the marinade.
Add: *cornstarch* to the sweet and sour sauce.
❀ Leave fillets whole. Broil 7 - 10 minutes. Arrange on top of vegetables. Make sweet and sour sauce. Spoon sauce over fish. Serve.

Stir-fry Salmon with Fermented Black Beans

1 pound salmon fillets Remove bones, ⎤
    if any. Cut into about 1" cubes. | Combine well. Refrigerate
1 teaspoon salt | at least 1 hour or overnight.
½ teaspoon sugar ⎦

1 tablespoon fermented black beans Rinse and drain.
2 tablespoons minced white part of scallion
1 - 2 cloves garlic, minced
½ - 1 teaspoon grated ginger, p.13
1 tablespoon ginger wine, p.13
½ - 1 onion Slice thinly, lengthwise.
1 teaspoon oil
½ - ¾ cup fish or chicken broth
1 - 2 tablespoons thinly sliced or shredded green part of scallion

---

❀   Heat wok. Add oil, fermented black beans, minced white part of scallion, garlic and grated ginger. Stir-fry, using medium heat, till fragrant. Stir in ginger wine and onion. Stir-fry till onion is partly done, 2 - 3 minutes, adding broth 1 tablespoon at a time as needed.

❀   Add ¼ cup broth to wok. Bring to a boil. Add salmon. Gently stir-fry till salmon begins to flake, about 4 - 5 minutes, adding more broth as needed for gravy. Remove to a serving platter. Garnish with scallion. Serve.

Serves 3 - 4

Variations on the Theme

CHILI LOVERS: Add *1 - 2 fresh red or green chili peppers*, cut into thin rings, at the same time as onion.

Fish suitable for this recipe include: *Swordfish, tuna, bass, mahi-mahi, halibut, blue fish, cod, red snapper.*

STEAMED SALMON WITH FERMENTED BLACK BEANS

1 pound salmon fillets Remove small bones. Score skin side, ½" - ¾"
   deep, at 1" intervals, creating small "pockets."

1 tablespoon fermented black beans Rinse and drain.
1 - 2 tablespoons minced shallots
2 - 4 cloves garlic, minced
2 tablespoons ginger wine, p.13
1 tablespoon regular soy sauce
½ teaspoon sugar
½ teaspoon kosher salt or to taste
white pepper or to taste
1 teaspoon oil
2 - 3 tablespoons broth or water
2 - 4 scallions Slant-cut into thin slices.

❀   Line a 9" Pyrex pie plate, or a similar size deep, heatproof plate
with scallion. Place salmon on top.

❀   Heat wok. Add oil, fermented black beans, shallots and garlic.
Stir-fry till fragrant, using medium heat, adding broth or water 1
tablespoon at a time if needed to prevent burning. Stir in ginger wine,
soy sauce, sugar, salt and white pepper. Bring to boil. Remove from
heat. Fill salmon "pockets" with mixture.

❀   Steam (see p.186) 8 - 10 minutes or till salmon is just cooked.
Serve at once directly from plate used in steaming.

Serves 3 - 4

VARIATION ON THE THEME

STEAMED WHOLE SEA BASS WITH FERMENTED BLACK BEANS

Substitute: *whole sea bass* for the *salmon fillets.*
❀   Score fish on both sides. Fill fish "pockets" on both sides with
mixture. Steam 15 - 20 minutes or till fish is just cooked.

BROILED SALMON WITH GINGER & SCALLIONS

1 pound salmon fillets⎤ Rub salt all over salmon fillet. Refrigerate
2 - 3 teaspoons salt ⎦ at least 2 hours or preferably overnight.

1 - 3 tablespoons shredded fresh ginger
2 - 4 scallions Shred or slice thinly.

❀   Lightly brush both sides of salmon with oil. Place skin side down on a lightly oiled or non-stick baking pan.

❀   Broil on high, in the middle of the oven, for 5 minutes.

❀   Remove salmon from baking pan. Spread shredded ginger and scallions on baking pan to the size and shape of salmon fillet. Place salmon, skin side up, on top of ginger and scallions.

❀   Broil an additional 5 - 8 minutes or till salmon is just cooked. Serve immediately.

Serves 3 - 4

NOTE: This is a high-sodium dish. Balance it with low-sodium grain dishes and low-sodium vegetable dishes.

Cook as suggested above, the salmon skin is crispy and appeals to the Asian palate. If you do not like salmon skin for aesthetic reasons, you may wish to reverse the cooking order. First, broil skin side up; then broil skin side down.

CHILI SHRIMP WITH SNOW PEAS & BABY CORN

1 pound raw shrimp Shell, devein, wash and pat dry well.

½ teaspoon kosher salt
½ teaspoon sugar
1 teaspoon cornstarch
¼ - 2 teaspoons Asian chili sauce
white pepper to taste
few slices fresh ginger

Combine. Add shrimp and mix well. Marinate at ½ hour or overnight in the refrigerator.

6 - 8 ounces snow peas Wash. Remove ends and strings.
1 15-ounce can baby corn Drain. Rinse. Cut in smaller pieces if desired.
1 medium or large onion Cut into 6 or more wedges.
a few strips of red pepper
1 teaspoon oil
½ - 1 teaspoon minced garlic or to taste
1 - 2 fresh red or green chili peppers (optional) Cut into thin rings.
½ - 1 cup broth
kosher salt to taste

2 teaspoons cornstarch
1 tablespoon water

Combine in a small dish. Stir well before adding to wok.

❀ In a wok or large frying pan, bring ¼ cup broth to a boil, using high heat. Add snow peas, baby corn, onion and red pepper. Stir-fry till snow peas are slightly under desired doneness, 3 - 4 minutes for crisp-tender. Remove all vegetables and liquid to a platter.

❀ Add oil and garlic to wok. Stir-fry, using medium heat, till garlic is soft, about 2 - 3 minutes. Add shrimp and fresh chili peppers. Stir-fry till shrimp changes color, adding broth as needed to prevent burning. Add vegetables and more broth as needed for gravy. Bring to a boil. Thicken with cornstarch mixture. Add salt to taste. Serve.

Serves 3 - 4

Curry Shrimp

1 pound large raw shrimp Shell, devein, rinse and pat dry.
1 teaspoon oil
1 - 3 tablespoons curry powder or to taste
¼ - 2 teaspoons Asian chili sauce
1 teaspoon kosher salt or to taste
1 tablespoon minced shallots
2 - 3 cloves garlic, minced
1 - 2 tomatoes Peel. Discard seeds. Chop coarsely.
2 - 3 potatoes (preferably red skin) Peel. Cut into ¾" cubes.
1 onion Peel. Cut into ¾" chunks.
¾ - 1 cup broth

❋   In a large heavy pot, bring ¾ cup broth and potatoes to a boil. Cover and simmer till potatoes are nearly cooked.

❋   Heat wok. Add oil and curry powder. Stir-fry about 5 seconds, using medium heat. Add chili sauce, salt, shallots and garlic. Stir-fry about 2 minutes or till shallots and garlic are translucent, adding broth 1 tablespoon at a time to prevent burning. Add shrimp and tomatoes. Stir-fry till shrimp changes color and is well coated with curry mixture.

❋   Add shrimp and onion to potatoes. Mix well. Bring to boil. Simmer about 5 minutes or till shrimp and potatoes are cooked, adding more broth as needed for gravy. Serve with lots of rice.

Serves 3 - 4

Variation on the theme

Curry Fish

Substitute: *¾ pound cod, haddock or red snapper* for the *shrimp.*
          Cut fish into bite-sized pieces.

Rock Shrimp with Broccoli

¾ pound cleaned rock shrimp
½ teaspoon kosher salt, or to taste
½ teaspoon sugar
1 teaspoon cornstarch
¼ - 1 teaspoon grated fresh ginger
½ - 2 teaspoons puréed garlic

Combine and mix well. Marinate at least ½ hour or overnight in the refrigerator.

1 - 2 pounds broccoli florets Cut into bite-sized pieces. Place in a large container. Pour boiling water to cover. Stir and drain at once. Cool under cold running water. Drain well.
¾ - 1 cup broth
kosher salt to taste

1 tablespoon cornstarch
2 tablespoons water

Combine in a small dish. Stir well before adding to wok.

❀ In a wok or large frying pan, bring ¾ cup broth to a boil, using high heat. Add broccoli. Stir-fry till broccoli is slightly under desired doneness. Remove to platter, leaving liquid in wok.

❀ Bring liquid in wok to a boil. Add rock shrimp. Cook till just done, adding more broth as needed for gravy. Thicken with cornstarch mixture. Stir in broccoli. Add salt to taste. Serve.

Serve 3 - 4

Variations on the theme

CHILI LOVERS: Add *Asian chili sauce* or *Asian chili garlic sauce* any time during cooking.

Rock Shrimp with Asparagus

Substitute: *1 - 2 pounds asparagus* for the *broccoli.*
Peel asparagus (see p.26). Cut into 1 - 2" lengths.

VEGETABLES

91
Chinkiang Vinegar Cabbage
*Chinkiang Vinegar Napa
Cabbage*

92
Gai Lan with Garlic Oyster Sauce
*Sugar Snap Peas with
Garlic Oyster Sauce
Snow Pea Shoots with
Garlic Oyster Sauce
Baby Bok Choy with
Garlic Oyster Sauce
Lettuce with Garlic Oyster Sauce
Broccoli Rabe with
Garlic Oyster Sauce*

94
Bean Sprouts with Chinese Chives
*Savoy Cabbage with
Chinese Chives
Napa Cabbage with
Chinese Chives*

95
Stir-fry Vegetable Sticks

96
Lotus Root Salad
*Jicama Salad
Asparagus Salad
Daikon Salad*

98
English Cucumber Salad
Salad of Summer Squash

99
Braised Vegetable Kabobs With Ginger & Rice Vinegar Dressing
*Two Flowers with
Ginger & Rice Vinegar Dressing
Green Cabbage with
Ginger & Rice Vinegar Dressing
Brussels Sprouts with
Ginger & Rice Vinegar Dressing
Summer Salad
Napa, Tomato & Watercress Salad
with Macadamia Nuts*

102
Szechuan Eggplant

103
Chinese Long Beans in Black Bean Garlic Sauce
*Fresh Beans in
Black Bean Garlic Sauce
Asparagus in
Black Bean Garlic Sauce*

104
Braised Summer Squash with Dried Shrimp
*Braised Chinese Eggplant with
Dried Shrimp*

MONEY-SAVING, TIME-SAVING TIPS

Many of the vegetable dishes in this section can be made into a complete meal: add some cooked meat or cooked seafood and serve with noodles, pasta, rice or a loaf of crusty bread.

Serve noodles, pasta or rice on the side. Or arrange cooked vegetables and meat on top of noodles, pasta or rice on a serving platter.

How about tossing the noodles or pasta with the vegetables and meat?

Next time you are cooking noodles or pasta, make extra. Doesn't Napa, Tomato & Watercress Salad with Macadamia Nuts, p.101, tossed with cooked seafood and pasta sound just great for a light summer meal?

Revive wilted vegetables by immersing in cold water for at least 15 minutes.

Vegetables will keep longer and in better condition in the refrigerator if placed in a paper bag, or wrapped in paper towels before being put in a plastic bag.

If you're choosing between frozen vegetables and canned vegetables, go for the frozen vegetables. Thaw completely before stir-frying.

CHINKIANG VINEGAR CABBAGE

2 pounds green or Savoy cabbage Cut into ½" × 2" strips.
2 teaspoons vegetable oil
6 - 8 whole dried chili peppers
1 - 2 teaspoons Szechuan peppercorns
1½ teaspoons kosher salt
2 tablespoons brown sugar or to taste
2 tablespoons regular soy sauce
3 tablespoons Chinkiang vinegar
1 teaspoon sesame oil (optional)

❀ Heat wok. Add vegetable oil. Add chili peppers. Stir-fry till chili peppers turn black. Add peppercorns; stir-fry another 5 seconds. Add cabbage. Stir-fry till cabbage wilts, adding water 1 teaspoon at a time, if wok is dry, to prevent burning.

❀ Add salt, sugar and soy sauce. Stir-fry 3 - 5 minutes, till cabbage has lost its raw taste, but remains very crisp. Mix in vinegar and sesame oil. Transfer to a serving platter. Serve at room temperature.

VARIATION ON THE THEME

CHINKIANG VINEGAR NAPA CABBAGE

Substitute: *2 pounds napa cabbage* for the *green cabbage*.
Cut napa cabbage lengthwise into about ¾" wide strips.
Cut strips into 2" lengths.

Gai Lan with Garlic Oyster Sauce

(Chinese Broccoli with Garlic Oyster Sauce)

1½ pounds gai lan Wash well and drain. Cut into 2" lengths. Peel
   stems at root end if woody. Cut thick stems in half lengthwise to
   assure even cooking. White flowers are edible; do not discard.
4 quarts water
1 tablespoon sugar (optional)
2 teaspoons oil (optional)
½ teaspoon oil
1 - 4 cloves garlic, smashed and peeled
a thumb-size piece of fresh ginger, peeled and smashed
kosher salt to taste

1 - 2 tablespoons oyster sauce
white pepper to taste | Combine in a small dish.
1 teaspoon cornstarch | stir before adding to wok.
2 tablespoons chicken broth or water

❀ In a large pot, bring water to a boil, using high heat. Add sugar
and 2 teaspoons oil. Add gai lan; return to a boil. Parboil 3 - 5
minutes, using medium heat, or till desired doneness is reached.

❀ While water is heating, heat wok, using medium-low heat. Add
½ teaspoon oil, garlic and ginger, allowing garlic and ginger to
slowly steep and flavor the oil. Just before gai lan reaches desired
doneness, remove and discard garlic and ginger, if desired. Add
oyster sauce mixture to wok. Bring to a boil, stirring constantly till
sauce thickens. Drain gai lan well. Add to wok. Toss to coat well.
Add salt to taste. Serve at once.

Variations on the Theme

CHILI LOVERS: Add *Asian chili sauce* to taste to the oyster sauce
mixture.

GAI LAN WITH GARLIC OYSTER SAUCE (continued)

SUGAR SNAP PEAS WITH GARLIC OYSTER SAUCE

Substitute: *1 pound sugar snap peas* for the *gai lan.*
        Remove ends and strings from peas. Leave whole.
❀   Blanch 2 - 3 minutes.

SNOW PEA SHOOTS WITH GARLIC OYSTER SAUCE

If you are fortunate enough to have a fantastic garden of snow peas, try this dish. Keep in mind you are eating the pea shoots at the expense of your snow peas. Gather the shoots just as they are emerging and before any flowers appear.
Substitute: *8 - 12 ounces snow pea shoots* for the *gai lan.*
        Wash and drain well. Leave whole.
❀   Blanch 1 - 2 minutes.

BABY BOK CHOY WITH GARLIC OYSTER SAUCE

Substitute: *1½ pounds baby bok choy* for the *gai lan.*
        Leave baby bok choy whole or cut in half lengthwise.
❀   Blanch 3 - 5 minutes if whole, 2 - 3 minutes if halved.

LETTUCE WITH GARLIC OYSTER SAUCE

Substitute: *1½ pounds iceberg, romaine or Boston lettuce* for the
        gai lan.
❀   Blanch 1 - 2 minutes.

BROCCOLI RABE WITH GARLIC OYSTER SAUCE

If you tried broccoli rabe but did not like the slightly bitter flavor, give it a second chance with this recipe.
Substitute: *1½ pounds broccoli rabe* for the *gai lan.*
        Cut into 2 - 3 lengths. Peel stems at root end if they
        appear woody.
❀   Blanch 3 - 5 minutes.

BEAN SPROUTS WITH CHINESE CHIVES

¾ pound bean sprouts Wash. Drain well.
¼ pound Chinese chives Wash. Drain well. Cut into 1½" lengths.
thumb-size piece of ginger Peel and smash.
1 teaspoon kosher salt or to taste
1 teaspoon oil

❀   Heat wok. Add oil and ginger. Stir-fry, using medium heat, till ginger is lightly browned. Remove and discard ginger. Turn heat to high, add salt, bean sprouts and chives. Stir-fry till desired doneness is reached, 1 - 3 minutes for bean sprouts to lose their raw taste. Add salt to taste. Serve.

VARIATIONS ON THE THEME

SAVOY CABBAGE WITH CHINESE CHIVES

Substitute: *¾ - 1 pound shredded Savoy cabbage* for the *bean
           sprouts.*
Add: *1 - 2 tablespoons regular soy sauce or to taste*
❀   Add soy sauce at the same time as cabbage.
Reduce to: *½ teaspoon kosher salt or to taste.*

NAPA CABBAGE WITH CHINESE CHIVES

Substitute: *¾ - 1 pound napa cabbage* for the *bean sprouts.*
           Cut napa cabbage lengthwise into about ¼" inch wide
           strips. Cut strips into 2" lengths.
Add: *1 or more fresh red chili peppers.*
    Cut into thin rings or matchstick strips.
❀   Add chili peppers at the same time as cabbage.

STIR-FRY VEGETABLE STICKS

1 - 2 carrots Cut into finger-size sticks.
1 zucchini Cut into finger-size sticks.
1 yellow squash Cut into finger-size sticks.
4 - 6 ounces Chinese celery Remove and discard leaves. Cut stems
    into 2" lengths.
½ - 1 green pepper Cut into finger-size strips.
½ - 1 can small baby corn Drain. Leave whole.
½ - 1 cup vegetable or chicken broth or water
1 - 2 tablespoons ginger wine, p.13
1 teaspoon kosher salt or to taste
½ teaspoon pulverized Chinese rock sugar or brown sugar (optional)
1 - 2 tablespoons regular soy sauce or to taste (optional)

❀   In a wok or large frying pan, bring ¼ cup broth to a boil, using
high heat. Add carrot sticks. Stir-fry 1 - 2 minutes. Add ginger wine,
salt, sugar and remaining vegetables. Stir-fry till vegetables reach
desired doneness, about 5 minutes if you like them crisp, adding more
broth as needed to prevent burning. Stir in soy sauce. Add salt to taste.
Serve.

Suggestions for additional vegetables: *kohlrabi, jicama, celery,
eggplant, asparagus, green beans, chayote, snow peas.*

VARIATION ON THE THEME

CHILI LOVERS: Add *1 - 2 fresh red* or *green chili peppers*, cut into
thin rings, or *Asian chili sauce* to taste when adding remaining vegetables.

LOTUS ROOT SALAD

1 section lotus root (about ¾ pound) Peel. Cut into about ⅛" thick
   slices. Immerse in cold water to prevent discoloration.
2 quarts water

*1½ tablespoons pulverized Chinese rock
   sugar or granulated white sugar*
1 - 2 tablespoons rice vinegar or to taste
1 tablespoon regular soy sauce
½ teaspoon kosher salt
1 teaspoon sesame oil (optional)

Combine in a small
dish. Mix well to
dissolve sugar and salt.
This is the sauce.

1 - 3 cups Chinese parsley leaves. Wash and dry well.
1 - 2 teaspoons toasted black sesame seeds

❀   In a 3 - 4 quart pot, bring 2 quarts water to a boil, using high
heat.

❀   Drain lotus root and add to boiling water. Return to a boil.
Lower heat to medium low; simmer lotus root for 3 minutes. Drain
at once and cool under cold running water. Drain and pat dry each
slice.

❀   Place dried lotus root in a mixing bowl. Add sauce and mix well.
Refrigerate till ready to use.

❀   Scatter Chinese parsley on a serving platter. Drain lotus root.
Arrange on top of Chinese parsley. Sprinkle on black sesame seeds.
Serve.

Makes about 45 - 50 slices

Wokking Your Way to Low Fat Cooking

Variations on the theme

Jicama Salad

Substitute: *¾ pound jicama* for the *lotus root*.
Peel jicama. Cut into about ⅛" thick slices, or shred.
❀ Parboil 2 minutes.

Asparagus Salad

Substitute: *¾ pound - 1 pound asparagus* for the *lotus root*.
Peel asparagus (see p.26). Remove scales. Leave whole or cut in halves.
❀ Parboil 1 minutes.
Add: *2 - 3 red radishes*.
Shred red radishes.
❀ Do not parboil. Add shredded radishes to mixing bowl with asparagus.

Daikon Salad

Substitute: *¾ pound daikon* for the *lotus root*.
Peel daikon. Cut into finger-sized logs or ¼" thick slices.
❀ Parboil logs for 3 minutes; parboil slices for 2 minutes.
Add: *1 - 2 fresh red or green chili peppers*.
Cut chili peppers into thin rings.
❀ Do not parboil. Add chili peppers to mixing bowl with daikon.

ENGLISH CUCUMBER SALAD

1 English cucumber Cut into very thin slices.
2 - 3 teaspoons kosher salt
2 - 3 tablespoons pulverized Chinese rock sugar or white sugar
¼ cup rice vinegar or to taste

❀　Combine cucumber slices and salt in a bowl. Let stand at room temperature for 15 minutes.

❀　Squeeze cucumber slices to extract as much liquid as possible. Place in a serving bowl. Add sugar and vinegar. Mix well. Serve.

VARIATIONS ON THE THEME

Add: *1 fresh red chili pepper*.
　　　Cut chili pepper into very thin rings.
❀　Add chili pepper at the same time as sugar and vinegar.

SALAD OF SUMMER SQUASH

Substitute: *1 small zucchini* and *1 small yellow squash* for the
　　　　　cucumber.
　　　　　Cut into about ⅛" thick slices.
Add: *1 small red or yellow onion*.
　　　Cut into about ⅛" thick slices.
❀　Add onion the same time as sugar and vinegar.
Garnish with: *1 - 2 tablespoons dried cranberries*.

Braised Vegetable Kabobs with Ginger & Rice Vinegar Dressing

12 small mushrooms Cut off stems. Flute caps (optional).
1 - 2 large carrots Peel and cut into 12 ¾" pieces.
1 pound daikon Peel and cut into 12 1" cubes.
2 - 3 very small yellow squash Cut into 12 1" pieces.
2 - 3 very small zucchini Cut into 12 1" pieces.
tomato slices for garnish
Chinese parsley for garnish
12 6 - 8" bamboo skewers
4 cups fat-free chicken broth

1 - 2 tablespoons very thinly
  shredded fresh ginger
¼ - ½ cup rice vinegar
1½ teaspoons kosher salt or to taste
2 teaspoons sugar or to taste

Combine in a small dish. This is the Ginger & Rice Vinegar Dressing.

❀   In a wok or saucepan, bring broth to a boil. Cook each vegetable separately to slightly under desired doneness. Cool at room temperature.

❀   Thread vegetables onto bamboo skewers. Arrange on serving platter. Garnish platter with tomato slices and Chinese parsley.

❀   Spoon desired amount of dressing over kabobs and serve.

Makes 12 kabobs

NOTE: Ginger & Rice Vinegar Dressing makes a great low-calorie salad dressing. If you do not like shredded ginger on your salad, simply strain the dressing before adding it to your salad.

Variations on the Theme

CHILI LOVERS: Add thinly shredded *red* and/or *green chili peppers,* to taste, to the Ginger and Rice Vinegar Dressing.

Two Flowers with Ginger & Rice Vinegar Dressing

Substitute*: 1 pound broccoli florets* and *1 pound cauliflower* for the *vegetables.*

Cut broccoli florets into bite-sized pieces. Place in a large container. Cover with boiling water. Stir. Drain. Cool under cold running water. Drain.

Cut cauliflower into bite-sized pieces.

Use: *½ cup chicken broth or water*

❀ In a wok or large frying pan, bring broth to a boil, using high heat. Add broccoli and cauliflower. Stir-fry till slightly under desired doneness. Remove to a serving platter or bowl, discard any cooking liquid. Toss vegetables with Ginger & Rice Vinegar Dressing to taste. Serve hot or cold.

Green Cabbage with Ginger & Rice Vinegar Dressing

Substitute: *1 - 2 pounds green cabbage* for the *broccoli* and *cauliflower* in the recipe above.

Cut cabbage into ½" wide pieces.

Brussels Sprouts with Ginger & Rice Vinegar Dressing

Substitute*: 1 - 2 pounds Brussels sprouts* for the *broccoli* and *cauliflower* in the recipe above.

Trim off mature leaves from Brussels sprouts. Wash and drain. Cut small sprouts in halves, large ones in quarters.

Add*: 1 teaspoon sugar*.

❀ Bring 2 - 3 quarts of water to a boil. Add sugar. Add Brussels sprouts. Return to a boil. Simmer 3 minutes or till slightly under

BRAISED VEGETABLE KABOBS WITH GINGER & RICE VINEGAR DRESSING (continued)

desired doneness. Drain well. Toss with Ginger & Rice Vinegar Dressing to taste. Serve.

SUMMER SALAD

Combine: *lettuce (butterhead, romaine), radicchio and escarole.*
Toss with: *Ginger & Rice Vinegar Dressing, p.99,* to taste.

NAPA, TOMATO & WATERCRESS SALAD WITH MACADAMIA NUTS

1 pound napa cabbage Cut cabbage lengthwise into ½" wide strips.
    Cut strips into 1½" lengths.
1 bunch watercress Use both leaves and stems. Cut into shorter
    lengths if desired. Discard any discolored leaves and mature
    stems.
4 - 6 plum tomatoes Skin and seed. Cut lengthwise into ¼" wide
    strips.
¼ cup coarsely chopped macadamia nuts

❀ Blanch napa cabbage in a large pot of boiling water for 2 - 3 minutes, or until it loses its raw taste. Drain and cool at once under cold running water. Drain and pat dry well.
❀ Blanch watercress for 1 minute. Drain and cool at once under cold running water. Drain and pat dry well. Toss to loosen.
❀ Arrange napa cabbage, watercress and tomatoes attractively on salad plates. Add Ginger & Rice Vinegar Dressing, p.99, to taste. Sprinkle macadamia nuts on top of salad. Serve.

SZECHUAN EGGPLANT

¾ pound Chinese eggplant (4 - 5 eggplants) Remove and discard
   caps. Cut eggplants into finger-size logs.
1 teaspoon oil
1 - 3 cloves garlic, minced
¼ - 2 teaspoons Asian chili sauce or to taste
1 tablespoon ginger wine, p.13
2 tablespoons regular soy sauce
1 teaspoon kosher salt or to taste
1 teaspoon brown sugar
¼ - ½ cup vegetable or chicken broth or water
1 tablespoon Chinkiang vinegar
½ teaspoon sesame oil (optional)
1 scallion Slice into thin rings.
1 tablespoon toasted white sesame seeds

❊   Heat wok. Add oil and garlic. Stir-fry, using medium to medium-
low heat till garlic is soft, adding broth 1 tablespoon at a time to prevent burning. Stir in chili sauce.

❊   Add eggplant, ginger wine, soy sauce, salt and sugar. Increase
heat to medium-high. Stir-fry till eggplant is evenly coated, adding
broth 1 tablespoon at a time to prevent burning. Add 2 - 3 tablespoons
broth. Bring to a boil. Cover and simmer 3 - 4 minutes, or till eggplant
is soft and liquid is absorbed.

❊   Stir in vinegar and sesame oil. Transfer to a plate. Garnish with
scallion rings and sesame seeds. Serve hot or at room temperature.

CHINESE LONG BEANS IN BLACK BEAN GARLIC SAUCE

1 pound Chinese long beans Remove ends. Cut beans into 2" lengths.
1 - 3 teaspoons fermented black beans or to taste Rinse.
2 - 4 cloves garlic Smash, peel and mince.
1 teaspoon kosher salt or to taste
½ teaspoon brown sugar
1 tablespoon ginger wine, p.13
¼ - ½ cup broth or water
1 teaspoon oil

½ teaspoon cornstarch ⎤ Combine in a small dish. Stir before
2 teaspoons broth or water ⎦ adding to wok.

❀   Heat wok. Add fermented black beans, garlic and salt. Stir-fry till fragrant. Add beans, brown sugar and ginger wine. Stir-fry till beans change color, adding broth 1 tablespoon at a time, if wok seems dry, to prevent burning.

❀   Add about ¼ cup broth to beans. Bring to a boil. Cover and simmer 4 - 5 minutes or till beans reach desired doneness. Thicken with cornstarch mixture. Serve.

VARIATIONS ON THE THEME

FRESH BEANS IN BLACK BEAN GARLIC SAUCE

Substitute: *1 pound green, Italian* or *yellow wax beans* for the
                Chinese long beans.
                Leave beans whole or cut into shorter lengths.
Add: *¼ - 1 teaspoon Asian chili sauce or to taste.*
❀   Add chili sauce at the same time as the garlic.

ASPARAGUS IN BLACK BEAN GARLIC SAUCE

Substitute: *1 - 1½ pounds asparagus* for the *Chinese long beans.*
                Peel asparagus (see p.26). Cut into 2" lengths.

Braised Summer Squash with Dried Shrimp

1 pound zucchini ⎤ Cut into quarters lengthwise. Cut each
1 pound yellow squash ⎦ quarter into 2" lengths.

2 tablespoons Chinese dried shrimp Rinse and coarsely chop.
    Soak in ¼ cup warm water for at least 15 minutes.
2 - 4 cloves garlic, minced
1 tablespoon thinly sliced shallots
2 tablespoons ginger wine, p.13
white pepper to taste
1 teaspoon kosher salt or to taste
1 teaspoon oil
1 - 2 tablespoons coarsely chopped Chinese parsley

1½ teaspoons cornstarch ⎤ Combine. Stir before adding
1 tablespoon water ⎦ to wok.

❀   Drain shrimp. Strain and reserve liquid.

❀   Heat wok. Add oil, drained shrimp, garlic and shallots. Stir-fry,
using medium to medium-low heat till shrimp is fragrant and garlic
is lightly browned. Add zucchini, yellow squash, ginger wine, white
pepper and salt. Mix well. Transfer all to a heavy pot.

❀   Add reserved liquid (discard any sediment) to squash. Bring to
a boil. Cover and simmer till squash is tender, about 10 minutes.
Thicken with cornstarch mixture. Stir in Chinese parsley. Serve.

Variation on the Theme

Braised Chinese Eggplant with Dried Shrimp

Substitute: *1¼ - 1½ pounds Chinese eggplant* for the *zucchini* and
          yellow squash.
          Remove and discard eggplant caps. Cut eggplants into ¼"
          thick slices.
Add: *1 tablespoon dark soy sauce*
   1 teaspoon sugar.

Tofu & Mein Jin

107
Five-spice Pressed Tofu
Stir-fry

108
Vegetarian Lettuce Rolls
Vegetarian Lo Mein
Meatless Sandwich

110
Tofu & Beef Stir-fry
Tofu & Seafood Stir-fry
Tofu & Chicken Stir-fry

112
Kan Ssu Salad

113
Stir-fry Mein Jin

114
Mein Jin Stew
Braised Mein Jin with Daikon
Braised Mein Jin with Napa

116
Mein Jin in
Black Bean Garlic Sauce
Mein Jin with Bok Choy
Mein Jin with Chinese Eggplant

118
Mein Jin in Hoisin Sauce

Tofu & Mein Jin recipes in other sections of this book

155 Meatless Lo Mein
172 Five-spice Pressed Tofu Kabobs with Peanut Sauce

ABOUT TOFU

Tofu, also known as bean curd, is a high-protein product made from soybeans. Tofu is an excellent and inexpensive meat substitute. It is high in calcium, low in cholesterol and easy to digest.

In Asian cuisine, tofu is frequently combined with poultry, meat and seafood. Thus combined, the usable protein content of tofu is increased. Combining tofu with other ingredients gives additional texture to the finished dish.

The smooth custard-like texture of fresh tofu enjoyed by many tofu lovers is also the quality that many dislike. If you were turned off by fresh tofu, try pressed tofu. Pressed tofu has the consistency of mozzarella cheese and can be purchased seasoned or unseasoned. Seasoned pressed tofu is frequently referred to as five-spice pressed tofu, and is available with or without chili. Unseasoned pressed tofu is available already shredded and is referred to as kan ssu.

Store fresh tofu in the refrigerator, immersed in cold water, changing water daily, for up to 7 days. Store pressed tofu in its original package, in the refrigerator, for up to 7 days. Pressed tofu freezes well.

ABOUT MEIN JIN

Mein jin, also known as wheat gluten or vegetable steak, is made from gluten—plant proteins in wheat—extracted from wheat flour. Mein jin is low in fat and calories.

Mein jin is one of the essential ingredients in Buddhist cooking and is frequently referred to as "Buddha food."

Fresh mein jin is gray in color with a rubbery texture. It is frequently sold rolled like huge cigars in one-pound packages. Having no flavor of its own, mein jin picks up the flavor of the food it is cooked with. Fresh mein jin will keep up to 7 days in the refrigerator. Its also freezes well.

FIVE-SPICE PRESSED TOFU STIR-FRY

8 ounces five-spice pressed tofu, thinly sliced
1 cup blanched bite-sized broccoli florets
1 cup bite-sized cauliflower
½ cup thinly sliced carrots
½ cup orange or yellow pepper strips
3 - 5 fresh shiitake mushrooms Remove and discard stems; slice
    caps into ¼" thick strips.
1 small onion Cut into 4 - 6 lengthwise wedges.
1 - 2 cloves garlic, minced
3 - 4 slices ginger from ginger wine, p.13
1 teaspoon kosher salt or to taste
½ teaspoon sugar or to taste
white pepper to taste
1 tablespoon regular soy sauce or oyster sauce
1 tablespoon ginger wine, p.13
½ - 1 cup vegetable broth, chicken broth or water
1 teaspoon oil

2 teaspoons cornstarch⎤ Combine in a small dish.
1 tablespoon water   ⎦ Stir before adding to wok.

❀   Heat wok. Add oil, garlic and ginger. Stir-fry, using medium heat, till garlic is lightly browned. Add all the vegetables, salt, sugar, white pepper, soy sauce and ginger wine. Stir-fry, using high heat, for 5 minutes, adding broth 1 tablespoon at a time to prevent burning.

❀   Add tofu and broth as needed to make gravy. Bring to a boil. Simmer till vegetables reach desired doneness. Add salt to taste. Thicken with cornstarch mixture. Serve.

Serves 3 - 4

VEGETARIAN LETTUCE ROLLS

8 ounces five-spice pressed tofu with chili, shredded
6 - 8 Chinese dried mushrooms Soak in warm water for 30 minutes
    to soften. Remove and discard stems. Shred caps.
2 cups bean sprouts
1 cup 1" lengths Chinese celery or regular celery, shredded
½ cup 1" lengths Chinese chives or scallion
½ cup 1" lengths red pepper strips
½ cup 1" lengths yellow tomato strips
1 - 2 leaves napa cabbage Cut lengthwise into thin strips; cut strips
    into 1" lengths.
1 1.7 or 2-ounce package bean thread Soak in warm water for at
    least 30 minutes. Cut into 2" lengths.
1 teaspoon oil
1 - 2 cloves garlic, minced
1 teaspoon kosher salt or to taste
½ teaspoon brown sugar or to taste
white pepper to taste
Asian chili sauce to taste
1 tablespoon ginger wine, p.13
1 tablespoon brown bean sauce or *miso*
¼ cup broth or water
½ cup coarsely chopped Chinese parsley (optional)
1 - 2 heads Boston lettuce or other leaf lettuce Separate leaves but
    leave whole. Wash and dry well. Place on a serving platter.

❀ Heat wok. Add oil, garlic and mushrooms. Stir-fry, using medium heat, till garlic is lightly browned. Add all vegetables, salt, sugar, white pepper, chili sauce, ginger wine and bean sauce. Stir-fry 5 minutes, using high heat, adding broth 1 tablespoon at a time to prevent burning.

❀ Add tofu and remaining broth. Bring to a boil. Add bean thread. Return to a boil. Simmer till all the liquid has been absorbed. Stir in

VEGETARIAN LETTUCE ROLLS (continued)

Chinese parsley, add salt to taste. Remove to a serving platter. Place on table with platter of lettuce.

TO SERVE: Place a leaf of lettuce on your plate. Spoon 1 - 2 tablespoons of the tofu mixture onto the middle of the lettuce leaf. Roll and eat. This is a finger food.

VARIATIONS ON THE THEME

VEGETARIAN LO MEIN

Substitute: *1 pound fresh Chinese egg noodles* for the *lettuce.*
❀   Cook noodles in a large pot of boiling water for 7 minutes. Drain. Eliminate: *bean thread.*
Add: *2 teaspoons cornstarch* combined with *1 tablespoon water*
     2 tablespoons coarsely chopped roasted unsalted peanuts.
❀   Follow the first step of the original recipe. Then add tofu and remaining broth. Thicken with cornstarch mixture. Stir in noodles, Chinese parsley and peanuts. Add salt to taste. Serve.

MEATLESS SANDWICH

Substitute: *five-spice pressed tofu, with or without chili* for *meat*
          Leave whole or slice thinly.
❀   Spread a little mayonnaise and/or mustard on a slice of bread, top with five-spiced pressed tofu, lettuce and tomatoes. Top with another slice of bread. Enjoy.

NOTE: Five-spiced pressed tofu is a cooked product and can be eaten as is from the package.

TOFU & BEEF STIR-FRY

8 - 10 ounces fresh tofu Cut tofu into ¾" cubes. Place in a colander to drain while preparing other ingredients.

½ pound lean sirloin steak Remove and discard all visible fat. Cut meat, across the grain, into about ⅛" thick slices.

2 teaspoons cornstarch *1 tablespoon ginger wine, p.13* *few slices ginger from ginger wine* *2 teaspoons dark soy sauce* *¾ teaspoon brown sugar* *dash white pepper or to taste*	Combine. Add beef. Mix well. Marinate at least ½ hour at room temperature or overnight in the refrigerator.

2 - 4 ounces snow peas Remove ends and strings.

2 - 4 ounces mushrooms Cut into ¼" thick slices.

1 - 2 ribs bok choy Cut into ½" thick slices.

1 large onion Peel and cut into 8 - 10 wedges.

1 carrot Peel and cut into thin slices.

½ - 1 cup chicken broth

1 teaspoon kosher salt or to taste

1 - 3 cloves garlic, finely minced

¼ - 2 teaspoons Asian chili garlic sauce (optional)

1 tablespoon oyster sauce or to taste

1 - 2 tablespoons thinly sliced or shredded scallions

½ - 1 teaspoon oil

❀ In a wok or large frying pan, bring 2 tablespoons broth to a boil, using high heat. Add salt, snow peas, mushrooms, bok choy, onion and carrot. Stir-fry till vegetables are slightly under desired doneness, 3 - 5 minutes for crisp-tender. Remove all vegetables and any remaining broth to a platter.

❀ Add oil and garlic to wok. Stir-fry, using medium heat, till garlic is lightly browned. Add chili garlic sauce and remaining ½ cup of broth. Bring to a boil, using high heat. Add beef. Stir-fry till beef changes color.

TOFU & BEEF STIR-FRY (continued)

❀ Add tofu. Gently stir-fry till tofu is heated through, adding more broth as needed for gravy. Stir in vegetables and oyster sauce. Add salt to taste. Remove to a serving platter, garnish with scallions and serve.

Serves 4 - 5

VARIATIONS ON THE THEME

TOFU & SEAFOOD STIR-FRY

Substitute: *4 ounces of shelled and deveined shrimp* and *4 ounces of bay scallops* for the beef
2 teaspoons of regular soy sauce for the *dark soy sauce*
½ pound jicama and *¾ - 1 pound asparagus* for the *snow peas, mushrooms* and *bok choy.*
Peel jicama. Cut into about 2"× ½"×⅛" thick slices.
Peel asparagus. Cut into about 2" lengths.

TOFU & CHICKEN STIR-FRY

Substitute: *½ pound chicken breast* for the *beef*
6 - 8 ounces blanched bite-sized broccoli florets for the *snow peas.*

KAN SSU SALAD
(Shredded Pressed Tofu Salad)

8 ounces kan ssu Blanch in boiling water for 20 seconds. Rinse and
cool under cold running water. Drain well. Cut into shorter
lengths, if desired.

4 ounces snow peas Remove ends and strings. Blanch in boiling
water for 10 seconds. Rinse and cool under cold running water.
Drain well. Pat dry. Shred.

1 carrot Peel and cut into match stick-sized pieces.

½ - 1 small red onion Cut into thin lengthwise strips.

¼ - ½ cup coarsely chopped Chinese parsley (optional)

1 - 3 teaspoons toasted black or white sesame seeds

2 tablespoons rice vinegar or to taste *1 - 2 tablespoons regular soy sauce* *1 teaspoon pulverized Chinese rock sugar* * or white sugar* *1 teaspoon Asian sesame oil* *¼ - 2 teaspoons Asian chili sauce (optional)*	Combine in a small dish. This is the dressing.

4 - 6 leaves of leaf lettuce Wash. Pat dry well. Break each into 4 or
5 pieces.

8 small pitas Cut each pita into 2 half-moons.

1 - 2 tablespoons hoisin sauce Place in a small sauce dish.

❀ Placed sliced pita on a damp steamer cloth or damp cheesecloth.
Steam (see p.186) on high heat, 5 - 7 minutes or till pliable.

❀ On a serving platter or serving bowl, combine blanched kan ssu,
snow peas, carrot, onion, Chinese parsley and sesame seeds. Toss
with dressing to taste.

TO SERVE: Brush a bit of hoisin sauce on the inside of a steamed
pita. Place a piece of lettuce inside, leaving the leaf edge extending
past the edge of the pita. Fill with 1 - 2 tablespoons of the Kan Ssu
Salad. Enjoy.

Serves 4 - 6

STIR-FRY MEIN JIN

8 ounces mein jin Cut each roll in half lengthwise, then slant-cut into about ¼" thick slices.

2 - 4 Chinese dried mushrooms Soak in warm water ½ hour to soften. Discard stems. Shred caps.

8 ounces Chinese celery Wash well. Remove and discard leaves. Cut stems into 2" lengths (or *regular celery* slant-cut into thin slices).

1 small yellow squash Cut into 3 - 4 lengthwise strips, Cut strips into thin slices.

1 - 2 carrots Cut in half lengthwise, then slant-cut into thin slices.

1 onion Cut into thin lengthwise strips.

1 cup 1" lengths Chinese chives or scallions

1 - 2 teaspoons oil

1 - 2 cloves garlic, minced

¼ - 2 teaspoons Asian chili sauce or to taste (optional)

1 teaspoon kosher salt or to taste

½ teaspoon sugar or to taste

¼ teaspoon white pepper or to taste

2 tablespoons ginger wine, p.13

1 tablespoon mushroom soy sauce

1 tablespoon oyster sauce or to taste (optional)

½ - 1 cup vegetable or chicken broth

2 teaspoons cornstarch⎤ Combine in a small dish. Stir
1 tablespoon water ⎦ before adding to wok.

❁   Heat wok. Add oil, garlic and mushrooms. Stir-fry, using medium heat, till mushrooms are fragrant. Stir in Asian chili sauce, salt, sugar, white pepper, ginger wine and soy sauce. Add mein jin. Stir-fry, using medium-high heat, till mein jin is well coated, adding broth 1 table-spoon at a time to prevent burning.

❁   Add all vegetables. Stir-fry till vegetables reach desired done-ness, adding broth as needed for gravy. Bring to a boil. Stir in oyster sauce. Thicken with cornstarch mixture. Add salt to taste. Serve.

Serves 3 - 4

MEIN JIN STEW

1 pound mein jin Slant-cut into ¾" thick slices.
1 - 3 teaspoons oil
1 onion, coarsely chopped
2 - 4 shallots, coarsely chopped
1 - 3 cloves garlic, minced
2 tablespoons ginger wine, p.13
1 tablespoon mushroom soy sauce
1 teaspoon brown sugar
1 teaspoon salt or to taste
1 - 2 carrots Cut into ¼" thick slices.
½ - 1 can straw mushrooms, drained and rinsed
1 cup pearl onions or *2 onions cut into chunks*
2 - 4 ounces snow peas Remove ends and strings.
a few strips yellow pepper
1 scallion Slant-cut.
1 - 2 cups vegetable or chicken broth
1 tablespoon oyster sauce (optional)

1 tablespoon cornstarch ⎤ Combine in a small dish.
2 tablespoons water ⎦ Stir before adding to pot.

❀ Heat wok. Add oil, chopped onion and shallots. Stir-fry, using medium to medium-high heat, till onion and shallots are browned but not burnt; this will take 5 - 10 minutes. Add garlic, stir-fry till garlic is translucent. Add mein jin, wine, soy sauce, sugar and salt. Stir-fry till all the liquid is absorbed. Transfer to a heavy pot.

❀ Add 1 cup broth to wok. Swirl broth and scrape the surface of the wok to release all the flavors that got stuck to the wok. Pour broth into pot with mein jin, adding enough broth to cover mein jin. Bring to a boil. Cover and simmer 30 minutes.

❀ Add carrots, straw mushrooms and pearl onions. Bring to a boil. Boil 5 minutes.

MEIN JIN STEW (continued)

❀   Add snow peas and yellow pepper. Boil another 3 minutes. If the stew seems too soupy, turn heat to high to reduce liquid. Thicken with cornstarch mixture. Stir in scallion and oyster sauce. Add salt to taste. Serve.

Serves 4 - 6

VARIATIONS ON THE THEME

CHILI LOVERS: Add *1 or more fresh red or green chili peppers*, whole or sliced, at the same time as broth. Or add *Asian chili sauce* to taste at the same time as the wine.

BRAISED MEIN JIN WITH DAIKON

Substitute: *1 pound daikon* for the *straw mushrooms, pearl onions snow peas* and *yellow pepper*.
          Peel daikon. Cut into 1" cubes.
          Cut carrots (from original recipe) into 1" chunks.
Add: *1 - 2 whole star anise*
     a thumb-sized piece of dried tangerine peel Soak in warm water at least 30 minutes to soften. Scrape away and discard the softened pith. Shred the peel.
❀   Add daikon, carrots, star anise and tangerine peel at the same time as broth. Simmer till daikon and carrots are tender, about 45 minutes.

BRAISED MEIN JIN WITH NAPA CABBAGE

Substitute: *1¼ - 2 pounds napa cabbage* for the *straw mushrooms, pearl onions, snow peas* and *yellow pepper*.
          Cut napa cabbage into 1" long pieces.
Eliminate: *2 teaspoons cornstarch* and *1 tablespoon water*.
Add: *2 - 4 sheets Tianjin green bean starch sheet*
     Soak in warm water for 30 minutes. Cut to desired lengths.
     1 - 3 tablespoons coarsely chopped Chinese parsley.
❀   Add napa cabbage at the same time as mein jin. Add bean sheets at the same time as the carrots. Stir in Chinese parsley and serve.

MEIN JIN IN BLACK BEAN GARLIC SAUCE

8 ounces mein jin Cut each roll in half lengthwise, then slant-cut into about ¼" thick slices.

1 - 1½ pounds broccoli Cut florets into bite-sized pieces. Peel stems and cut into bite-sized pieces. Place all the broccoli in a large container. Cover with boiling water. Stir. Drain. Cool under cold running water. Drain well.

½ cup sliced carrots

1 onion Cut into 4 - 6 lengthwise wedges.

1 - 2 teaspoons oil

1 tablespoon minced garlic or to taste

1 - 2 tablespoons fermented black beans Rinse and drain.

½ teaspoon grated fresh ginger or to taste

¼ - 2 teaspoons Asian chili sauce or to taste (optional)

1 teaspoon kosher salt or to taste

1 teaspoon brown sugar or to taste

¼ teaspoon white pepper or to taste

2 tablespoons ginger wine, p.13

1 tablespoon mushroom soy sauce

1 tablespoon oyster sauce or to taste (optional)

½ - 1 cup vegetable or chicken broth

2 teaspoons cornstarch⎤ Combine in a small dish. Stir
1 tablespoon water　　⎦ before adding to wok.

❉   In a wok or large frying pan, bring ¼ cup broth to a boil, using high heat. Add broccoli, carrots and onion. Stir-fry till vegetables are slightly under desired doneness, about 3 minutes for crisp-tender. Remove vegetables and broth to a platter.

❉   Heat wok. Add oil, garlic, fermented black beans, ginger and chili sauce. Stir-fry, using medium heat, till fragrant, 2 - 3 minutes. Stir in salt, sugar, white pepper, ginger wine and soy sauce. Add mein jin. Stir-fry, using medium-high heat, till mein jin is well coated, adding broth 1 tablespoon at a time to prevent burning.

MEIN JIN IN BLACK BEAN GARLIC SAUCE (continued)

❀ Add broth as needed for gravy. Bring to a boil. Simmer 5 minutes.

❀ Add all vegetables. Stir-fry till vegetables reach desired doneness. Bring to a boil, stir in oyster sauce. Thicken with cornstarch mixture. Add salt to taste. Serve.

Serves 3 - 4

VARIATIONS ON THE THEME

MEIN JIN WITH BOK CHOY

Substitute: *1 - 2 pounds bok choy* for the *broccoli*.
    Wash bok choy well. Slant-cut into ½" thick slices.
❀ Stir-fry bok choy in 2 tablespoons of broth instead of ¼ cup.
NOTE: Bok choy is a vegetable with high water content. You may wish to increase the cornstarch to 1 tablespoon.

MEIN JIN WITH CHINESE EGGPLANT

Substitute: *1 pound Chinese eggplants* for the *broccoli*.
    Remove and discard caps. Cut in half lengthwise, then slant-cut into ½" thick slices.

MEIN JIN IN HOISIN SAUCE

8 ounces mein jin Cut each roll in half lengthwise,
      then slant-cut into about ¼" thick slices.
½ - 1 green pepper, cut into strips
½ - 1 red pepper, cut into strips
½ - 1 yellow or orange pepper, cut into strips
½ teaspoon kosher salt or to taste
½ teaspoon brown sugar
1 tablespoon ginger wine, p.13
1 tablespoon regular soy sauce
2 - 3 tablespoons hoisin sauce
½ - 1 cup vegetable or chicken broth
1 - 2 teaspoons oil
½ cup roasted unsalted cashew nuts

2 teaspoons cornstarch ⎤ Combine in a small dish.
1 tablespoon water   ⎦ Stir before adding to wok.

❋   In a wok or frying pan, bring 2 tablespoons broth to a boil, using
high heat. Add salt and peppers. Stir-fry till peppers are heated
through, about 2 minutes. Remove peppers and any remaining broth
to a serving platter.

❋   Add oil and mein jin to wok. Stir fry, using medium-high to
high heat, till mein jin is lightly browned. Stir in wine and soy sauce;
stir-fry till liquid is absorbed. Add hoisin sauce. Mix well. Add broth
as needed for gravy. Bring to a boil. Thicken with cornstarch mixture.
Serve.

Serve 3 - 4

Soups

121
Basic Chicken Broth
Pork Broth

122
Fish Broth
Seafood Broth

123
Beef &
Chinese Parsley Soup
Chicken & Chinese Parsley Soup

124
Egg Drop Soup
Chicken Egg Drop Soup
Tofu Egg Drop Soup

125
Cream of
Winter Melon Soup
Cream of Daikon Soup
Cream of Pumpkin Soup

126
Shrimp Wonton Soup
Chicken Wonton Soup
Veal Wonton Soup
Beef Wonton Soup
Seafood Wonton Soup

130
Beef & Spinach Soup
Beef & Swiss Chard Soup
Beef & Broccoli Rabe Soup
Chicken & Spinach Soup

132
Crab, Scallop &
Sweet Corn Chowder
Chicken &
Sweet Corn Chowder
Tofu & Sweet Corn Chowder

134
Meatball Soup with
Vegetables
(Meatball Soup with
Vegetables & Noodles)
Turkey Balls Soup

SOUP RECIPES IN OTHER SECTIONS OF THIS BOOK

MONEY-SAVING, TIME-SAVING TIPS

Freeze broth in freezer containers or freezer bags in family-sized or individual-sized portions. Label and date.

Freeze broth in ice cube trays. To prevent broth cubes from having an unpleasant freezer taste, transfer broth cubes to a freezer bag or freezer container once they become frozen. Label and date. When a recipe calls for a small amount of broth, all you have to do is dissolve the number of cubes needed.

If time does not permit or you simply do not have enough bones to make broth, freeze bones as they become available. Make broth when sufficient ingredients are collected and/or time permits.

BASIC CHICKEN BROTH

4 - 5 pounds chicken parts or chicken bones with some meat on them
   Rinse well under cold running water to get rid of any blood.
cold water
2 teaspoons kosher salt or to taste
a thumb-size piece of ginger Peel and smash.
2 - 3 scallions
½ - 1 teaspoon peppercorns
1 carrot (optional) Coarsely chop.

❀   Place chicken in a large heavy stockpot. Cover with cold water. Add salt. Bring to a boil, uncovered, using high heat. To prevent broth from boiling over, reduce the heat at near boil. Skim the broth as necessary till the surface is clear.

❀   Add ginger, scallions, peppercorns and carrot. Bring to a boil. Lower heat to a slow simmer and cover pot. Simmer 3 - 6 hours. DO NOT stir and DO NOT allow broth to come to a rolling boil. Stirring and allowing broth to boil vigorously will result in cloudy broth.

❀   Strain broth using a fine sieve or a strainer lined with several layers of damp cheesecloth. Cool overnight in the refrigerator, if possible. Remove and discard fat that solidifies on surface. Keeps up to 3 days in the refrigerator. Freeze for longer storage.

Makes about 4 quarts

VARIATION ON THE THEME

For a richer broth and a different taste, add some pork bones at the same time as the chicken bones.

PORK BROTH

Substitute: *pork bones* for the *chicken bones*.

FISH BROTH

2 - 3 pounds fish heads and fish bones Rinse well under cold running
    water to get rid of any blood. Cut into smaller pieces, if desired.
1 - 2 teaspoons oil
a thumb-size piece of ginger Peel and smash.
1 small onion Coarsely chop.
1 scallion
2 tablespoons Chinese rice wine or pale dry sherry
2 teaspoons kosher salt or to taste
about 5 quarts water

❀ Heat wok. Add oil, ginger and onion. Stir-fry over medium heat
till onion is lightly browned, about 5 minutes. Add fish heads and
bones and stir-fry another 2 - 3 minutes, or till fish begins to change
color. Transfer to a large heavy stockpot.

❀ Add scallion and wine to stockpot. Add cold water to cover.
Bring to a boil, uncovered, using medium-high heat. Lower heat to
simmer. Skim the broth as necessary till the surface is clear. Cover
pot. Simmer broth for 30 minutes. DO NOT stir and DO NOT allow
to boil vigorously.

❀ Strain broth, using a fine sieve or a strainer lined with several
layers of damp cheesecloth. If broth tastes weak, return strained broth
to a clean heavy stockpot. Bring to boil, using medium heat. Continue
to boil, uncovered, using medium to medium-low heat, to reduce the
broth and to give it a more concentrated flavor. Add salt to taste.

Makes about 3½ quarts

VARIATION ON THE THEME

SEAFOOD BROTH

Add: *raw shrimp shells* and *lobster shells.*
❀ Stir-fry with the fish heads and fish bones.

BEEF & CHINESE PARSLEY SOUP

6 - 8 ounces lean beef Cut across the grain into about 1½"× ½"×⅛" thick strips.
1 tablespoon cornstarch
2 teaspoons regular soy sauce
⎫ Combine. Add ginger juice (below) and mix well.

1 - 2 teaspoons grated ginger
1½ tablespoons water
⎫ Combine and mix well. Extract juice (see p.13). Add to beef.

4 cups chicken broth
1 - 2 cups coarsely chopped Chinese parsley
¼ cup matchstick-sized carrot sticks
¼ teaspoon white pepper or to taste
kosher salt to taste
few drops sesame oil (optional)
1 - 2 white parts of scallion Cut into thin rings.

❀ In a large saucepan, bring broth to a boil, using medium to medium-high heat. Stir broth using chopsticks (it is much easier) while adding beef. Continue stirring to separate each slice of beef. Bring to a boil.

❀ Stir in Chinese parsley, carrot sticks and white pepper. Bring to a boil. Remove from heat. Add salt to taste. Stir in sesame oil. Ladle into soup bowls. Garnish with scallion rings. Serve hot.

Serves 4

VARIATION ON THE THEME

CHILI LOVERS: Add *Asian chili oil* to taste at the same time as the sesame oil.

CHICKEN & CHINESE PARSLEY SOUP

Substitute: *6 - 8 ounces chicken breast* for the *beef.*

Egg Drop Soup

4 cups chicken broth
1 teaspoon regular soy sauce
2 large eggs Mix well to combine whites and yolks.
a few drops Asian sesame oil (optional)
kosher salt to taste
white pepper to taste
thinly sliced scallion rings for garnish

2 - 4 tablespoons cornstarch ⎤ Combine in a small dish. Mix
¼ - ½ cup chicken broth or water ⎦ well before adding to broth.

❈   In a large saucepan, bring broth and soy sauce to a boil, using medium heat. Stir in cornstarch mixture. Return to a boil.

❈   Lower heat to a simmer. Add eggs, slowly and in a thin stream, stirring constantly but gently. Remove from heat. Stir in sesame oil. Add salt and white pepper to taste. Ladle into soup bowls. Garnish with scallion rings. Serve.

Serves 4

Variations on the Theme

Chicken Egg Drop Soup

Add: *4 ounces chicken breast* Coarsely chop. ⎤
       2 tablespoons broth or water   ⎥
       1 teaspoon cornstarch   ⎬ Combine.
       2 teaspoons ginger wine, p.13   ⎦
❈   Stir into broth before adding cornstarch mixture.

Tofu Egg Drop Soup

Add: *4 - 8 ounces tofu* Cut into about ½" cubes.
❈   Stir into broth after adding cornstarch mixture.

CREAM OF WINTER MELON SOUP

3 - 4 pounds winter melon Peel. Remove and discard seeds. Cut
    into big chunks.
4 - 5 cups good-quality chicken broth
2 - 4 ounces Chinese Kin Hwa ham, country ham or prosciutto,
    minced
a few drops sesame oil (optional)
kosher salt to taste
white pepper to taste
very thin slices of carrot for garnish
1 - 2 scallions, sliced thinly or shredded

❀   Put winter melon and broth in a large heavy pot. Bring to a boil,
using high heat. Lower heat to a simmer. Cover pot and simmer till
winter melon is very soft, about 60 minutes.

❀   Purée winter melon, using a hand blender or food processor. Return broth and puréed winter melon to a boil. Stir in ham and sesame
oil. Add salt and white pepper to taste. Garnish with carrot slices and
scallion. Serve hot.

Serves 5 - 6

VARIATIONS ON THE THEME

CREAM OF DAIKON SOUP

Substitute: *2 - 2½ pounds daikon* for the *winter melon.*
                Peel daikon. Cut into about 1" chunks.

CREAM OF PUMPKIN SOUP

Substitute: *2 - 3 pounds calabaza* or *kabocha* for the *winter melon.*

Shrimp Wonton Soup

¾ pound raw shrimp Shell, devein and coarsely chop.
¼ cup coarsely chopped bamboo shoots
1 scallion Slice thinly.
3 - 5 dried Chinese mushrooms Soak ½ hour to
    soften. Discard any stems. Coarsely chop caps.
½ teaspoon kosher salt or to taste
¼ teaspoon sugar
2 teaspoons ginger wine, p.13
2 teaspoons regular soy sauce

Combine. This is the wonton filling.

1 - 2 pounds bok choy Wash and slant cut into ½" thick pieces.
1 carrot Thinly slice.
a few slices of scallion
½ pound ready-made thin wonton wrappers (about 45)
6 - 8 cups chicken broth

❀   Make wontons according to the instructions on page 129. Place on a dry plate and cover with a dry towel.

❀   In a large pot, bring about 3 quarts of water to a boil. Drop wontons into boiling water, stirring gently to prevent wontons from sticking together. Bring to a boil. Reduce heat to medium. Cook, uncovered, till wontons float to the top, about 5 minutes. Drain and cool wontons under cold running water. Drain again thoroughly. Wontons may be frozen at this point.

❀   Bring stock to a boil. Add vegetables and desired amount of wontons. Bring to a boil. Simmer till vegetables reach desired doneness and wontons are heated through. Serve.

Makes about 45 wontons

Variations on the Theme

Substitute: *snow peas, spinach, watercress, napa cabbage, Chinese kale, blanched broccoli, blanched Chinese broccoli, baby corn, cauli-*

SHRIMP WONTON SOUP (continued)

flower, fluted mushrooms, asparagus, Chinese chives or *any other vegetables you like,* alone or in any combination for the *bok choy.*

CHICKEN WONTON SOUP

Substitute: *½ pound ground chicken* for the *shrimp*
¼ cup coarsely chopped water chestnuts for the *bamboo shoot.*

VEAL WONTON SOUP

Substitute: *½ pound ground veal* for the *shrimp*
2 tablespoons each coarsely chopped carrots and *water chestnuts* for the *bamboo shoots.*

BEEF WONTON SOUP

Substitute: *½ pound very lean ground beef* for the *shrimp*
½ cup coarsely chopped and squeezed almost dry napa cabbage for the *bamboo shoots.*
Add to filling: *1 - 2 tablespoons chopped Chinese chives*
1 - 2 tablespoons chopped Chinese parsley
1 - 2 teaspoons oyster sauce or to taste
¼ - ½ teaspoon Asian chili sauce or to taste.

SEAFOOD WONTON SOUP

Substitute: *4 ounces each coarsely chopped scallops* and *lobster* for the *shrimp.*
Add to filling: *¼ teaspoon white pepper or to taste*
1 - 2 teaspoons oyster sauce or to taste
½ - 1 teaspoon fresh ginger juice (p.13) *or to taste*

SHRIMP WONTON SOUP (continued)

Freezing wontons

Method 1: Package drained and cooled cooked wontons into serving size or meal size portions. Label, date and freeze.

Method 2: Line a jelly roll pan or any large baking pan with plastic wrap. Arrange drained and cooled cooked wontons in one layer on top of plastic wrap, leaving a little space between wontons. Cover with plastic wrap and freeze. After wontons are frozen, place them in a freezer bag or freezer container, label, date and return to freezer. I prefer this method even though it is a bit more time-consuming, because when I am ready to use the wontons, I can take out as many or as few as I need for that particular meal.

Serving frozen wontons

For best results, thaw overnight in the refrigerator before adding to boiling broth.

Thawing in the microwave is acceptable, but thaw at a low temperature.

If you must cook the wontons frozen, place the frozen wontons in boiling broth, lower the temperature to a simmer and allow wontons to heat slowly. If you must stir the soup, do so very gently.

Saving not so pliable wonton wrappers

If your wonton wrappers appear dry and brittle around the edges, wrap a damp paper towel around the pack of wonton wrappers (keep them in their original package). Place in a plastic bag. Close with a twist-tie. Leave in the refrigerator overnight. This will freshen the wrappers, making them pliable again.

SHRIMP WONTON SOUP (continued)

Assembling soup wontons

1. Moisten 3 edges of a wonton wrapper with water.

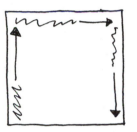

2. Place about 1 teaspoon filling in the middle of the unmoistened edge.

3. Fold edge one-third of the way over.

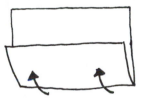

4. Fold over another one-third.

5. With thumbs and forefingers holding the two ends, press to seal and at the same time pull down, overlapping the two lower corners. Press the corners together to seal. (If corners do not seal, moisten them with a little water and press to seal.)

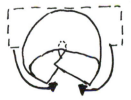

BEEF & SPINACH SOUP

6 - 8 ounces coarsely chopped lean beef ⎤ Combine. Add ginger
2 teaspoons cornstarch   juice (see below). Mix
½ teaspoon kosher salt   well. Refrigerate till
¼ teaspoon white pepper or to taste   ready to use. This can
1 tablespoon regular soy sauce   be done the day before.
a few drops Asian sesame oil (optional) ⎦

1 - 2 teaspoons grated fresh ginger ⎤ Combine. Extract juice (see
2 tablespoons broth or water   ⎦ p.13). Add juice to beef above.

½ cup cornstarch   ⎤ Combine in a small dish. Stir
¾ cup broth or water ⎦ before adding to pot.

10 - 12 ounces fresh spinach, leaves and stems Wash spinach well
    to get rid of any sand. Blanch in boiling water for 10 seconds.
    Drain. Cool under cold running water. Drain again and gently
    squeeze to remove excess water. Chop leaves and stems
    coarsely.
5 - 6 cups chicken broth
2 egg whites, lightly beaten till frothy
kosher salt to taste
white pepper to taste
1 - 2 scallions, white parts only Cut into thin rings.
very thin slices of carrots for garnish (optional)

❀   In a large saucepan, bring broth to a boil, using medium to
medium-high heat.

❀   Using chopsticks, loosen marinated chopped meat as much as
possible. Add to soup, stirring constantly to break up any lumps.
Bring to a boil.

❀   Pour in cornstarch mixture, stirring soup constantly. Bring to
a boil.

Beef & Spinach Soup (continued)

❀ Add blanched spinach. Bring to a boil. Stir in egg whites. Add salt and pepper to taste.

❀ Ladle into soup tureen or individual soup bowls. Garnish with scallion rings and carrot slices. Serve.

Serves 5 - 6

Variations on the Theme

Beef & Swiss Chard Soup

Substitute: *Swiss chard leaves* (save white stems for another use) for
       the *spinach*.
Add: *2 - 3 dried Chinese mushrooms* Soak in warm water for 30
    minutes. Remove and discard stems, shred caps.
❀ Add mushrooms to broth at the start of cooking.
 Garnish each bowl of soup with: *3 or more enoki mushrooms*.

Beef & Broccoli Rabe Soup

Substitute: *broccoli rabe* for the *spinach*
        1 1.7- ounce pack bean thread for the *½ cup cornstarch*
        Trim and peel root end of broccoli rabe if it seems tough.
        Blanch in boiling water for 1 minute.
        Soak bean thread in warm water for 15 minutes to soften.
        Cut into about 2" lengths.
❀ Add bean thread to broth at the same time as broccoli rabe.

Chicken & Spinach Soup

Substitute: *coarsely chopped chicken breast* for the *beef*

CRAB, SCALLOP & SWEET CORN CHOWDER

4 ounces bay scallops
½ teaspoon cornstarch
¼ teaspoon kosher salt
2 - 3 slices fresh ginger
dash of white pepper

Combine. Refrigerate till ready to use. This can be done the day before.

4 - 5 cups fish broth or chicken broth

2 ears sweet corn Cut corn from the cobs at about ⅔ the depth of the kernel. Scrape cob, using the dull side of a knife to extract the juice and heart of the kernel.

2 egg whites, lightly beaten till frothy

3 - 4 ounces cooked crabmeat

kosher salt to taste

white pepper to taste

2 tablespoons chopped Chinese Kin Hwa ham or country ham (optional)

2 - 3 tablespoons Chinese red vinegar
1 tablespoon thinly sliced scallion
1 - 2 tablespoons coarsely chopped
    Chinese parsley
1 tablespoon Asian chili sauce

Put in small sauce dishes. Place on table for use as condiments by individual diners.

❀ In a large heavy pot, bring broth to a boil. Add scallops. Return to a boil, using medium heat. Cook about 2 minutes. Add sweet corn. Return to boil. Simmer till scallops are cooked, about 2 more minutes.

❀ Stir in egg whites. Bring to a gentle simmer. Stir in cooked crabmeat and ham. Add salt and white pepper to taste. Ladle into a soup tureen or individual soup bowls. Serve hot. Diners can add condiments according to taste.

Serves 5 - 6

CRAB, SCALLOP & SWEET CORN CHOWDER (continued)

NOTE: A large can of cream-style corn may be substituted for the sweet corn.

VARIATIONS ON THE THEME

Substitute: *milk* or *milk and cream* for part of the *broth*.

CHICKEN & SWEET CORN CHOWDER

Substitute: *6 - 8 ounces coarsely chopped chicken breasts* for the
scallops and *crabmeat*.

TOFU & SWEET CORN CHOWDER

Substitute: *8 ounces of soft tofu* for the *scallops* and *crabmeat*
2 egg yolks for the *ham*.
Cut tofu into ¼" cubes or mash coarsely with a fork.
Scramble egg yolks and chop coarsely.
Add: *1 - 2 tablespoons green peas*
1 - 2 tablespoons coarsely chopped carrots.

MEATBALL SOUP WITH VEGETABLES

½ pound very lean ground pork
½ of a beaten egg
2 tablespoons tapioca starch or cornstarch   Combine. Mix well.
2 teaspoons ginger wine, p.13   Form into meatballs
1½ teaspoons regular soy sauce   about the size of
1 tablespoon minced shallots   grapes.
½ teaspoon kosher salt or to taste
dash of white pepper or to taste

1 - 2 pounds bok choy Cut into about ½" thick slices.
1 - 2 carrots Cut into thin slices or sticks.
4 - 6 ounces fresh mushrooms, sliced
2 ounces snow peas Remove ends and strings. Leave whole or cut
    in halves.
6 - 8 cups pork broth or chicken broth
1 scallions, thinly sliced
1 - 3 teaspoons regular soy sauce or to taste
kosher salt to taste
white pepper to taste
Asian chili sauce or chili oil Keep on table for diners to add to soup
    according to taste.

❀   Bring a large pot of water to a boil. Drop in meatballs. Bring to a boil. Simmer till meatballs float to the top, about 5 - 10 minutes. Drain and set aside.

❀   In a large heavy pot, bring broth to a boil. Add bok choy, carrots, mushrooms and snow peas. Bring to a boil. Simmer 5 minutes. Add meatballs. Simmer another 3 - 5 minutes or till vegetables reach desired doneness.

❀   Stir in scallion and soy sauce. Add salt and pepper to taste. Serve.

Serves 6 - 10

MEATBALL SOUP WITH VEGETABLES (continued)

VARIATIONS ON THE THEME

Boiled meatballs have a soft delicate texture. You can also bake these meatballs. Place them on a baking pan brushed with lemon juice or a non-stick baking pan. Bake at 350°F for 20 - 25 minutes. Both boiled and baked meatballs freeze well. Make extra for the freezer.

Suggestions for additional vegetables: Use alone or in any combination.

Choy sum (Chinese broccoli rabe) Yellow flowers are edible; do not discard. Cut into 1" - 2" lengths. Peel stems at root end if they appear woody. Cut thick stems in half lengthwise to assure even cooking.

Gai lan (Chinese broccoli) White flowers are edible; do not discard. Cut into 1" - 2" lengths. Peel stems at root end if they appear woody. Cut thick stems in half lengthwise to assure even cooking. Blanch in boiling water for 10 seconds. Drain and cool under cold running water if not adding to soup at once.

Baby corn Leave whole or cut into shorter lengths.

Straw mushrooms, peeled or unpeeled Cut large ones in half.

Broccoli Cut florets into bite-sized pieces. Peel stems and cut into bite-sized pieces. Blanch in boiling water for 5 seconds. Drain and cool under cold running water if not adding to soup at once.

Watercress, leaves and stems Wash and drain well. Leave whole or cut into shorter lengths.

Sze gwa (silk squash or angled luffa) Using a small sharp knife, remove and discard the ridges, leaving the green skin. Roll-cut into about 1" pieces.

Szechuan preserved vegetables For milder a taste, rinse before adding to soup.

The above are just some suggestions. As you can see, you can add just about any kind of vegetable you like.

MEATBALL SOUP WITH VEGETABLES & NOODLES

Add: *1 pound or more cooked noodles, any kind.*
Use: *1½ - 2 times the amount of broth called for in recipe.*
❀   Put hot cooked noodles in soup bowls. Ladle soup with some meatballs and vegetables on top of noodles. Serve.

TURKEY BALLS SOUP

Substitute*: ½ pound ground turkey for the ground pork*
             2 tablespoons flour for the tapioca starch.

Add: *1 tablespoon minced water chestnuts*   Combine with turkey
     1 teaspoon oyster sauce   and other ingredients.
     1 - 2 teaspoons minced Chinese parsley

Rice

MONEY-SAVING, TIME-SAVING TIPS

Store uncooked rice at room temperature in an airtight container. Adding a few bay leaves to the rice in the container will keep away any unwanted insects.

You can keep uncooked: white rice, indefinitely
                      brown rice, up to 6 months.

Cooked rice, brown and white, reheats well in the microwave. Save time by cooking extra. Cooked rice will keep for up to 6 days in the refrigerator.

Cooked brown rice also freezes well. Packaged in a freezer bag or freezer container, it will keep for up to 6 months in the freezer. Personally, I do not like reheated frozen white rice.

When cooking brown or white rice, Asians do not add salt or fat.

Use the amount of water given in the Boiled White Rice and Boiled Brown Rice recipes as a guide only. Add more water if you like softer rice, decrease the water if you prefer drier rice. A note to those who keep their uncooked rice in the refrigerator: depending on the kind of container your rice is stored in, you may need to add extra water when cooking.

1 cup uncooked white rice yields 3 cups cooked
1 cup uncooked brown rice yields 3 cups cooked.

ABOUT RICE

There is now a wide variety of rice available at the supermarket. Brown, white and glutinous. Long grain, medium grain and short grain. Then there is aromatic rice: Texmati, basmati, jasmine and so on.

Long grain rice, whether brown or white, has a dry texture. Cooked properly, the grains do not stick together.

Short grain rice has a softer and moister texture, and the cooked grains tend to stick together. This is the rice used for sushi.

The texture of medium grain rice falls between that of long and short grain rice. Experiment with the different types of rice to find your favorite.

Among the aromatic rice, basmati is the most aromatic and cooks the driest. There are different grades of basmati rice in the Indian stores. I recommend using the top grade.

Texmati rice is a cross between basmati and jasmine.

Jasmine rice, also known as Chinese rice and Thai rice, is mildly aromatic and cooks to a semi-dry texture.

Glutinous rice comes in long grain and short grain varieties. Whereas all the other raw rice is opaque and becomes white after cooking, uncooked glutinous rice is white and becomes opaque after cooking. Also known as sweet rice (it is used to make sweet pastries in Asian cuisine) and sticky rice (it is very sticky when cooked). Do not use as a substitute for regular rice. Glutinous rice is also used as a stuffing, especially for duck.

BOILED WHITE RICE

2 cups long or short grain white rice

_____

❀   Place rice in a 2 or 3-quart saucepan. Rinse till water runs clear.

❀   With index finger touching the SURFACE of the rice, add cold water to reach the first joint of the finger (about ⅞").

❀   Cook uncovered, using high heat, till most of the water has been absorbed (do not stir and do not lower the heat during this cooking period) and little craters begin to form on the surface of the rice. At this point, reduce heat to a simmer.

❀   Cover saucepan and simmer rice for 15 minutes. DO NOT peek during this simmering period. At the end of 15 minutes fluff rice and serve. If not serving at once, cover saucepan after fluffing and leave on warm range till ready to use.

Makes 6 cups

NOTE: Fingertip should be touching the SURFACE of the rice not through to the bottom of the saucepan.
Stirring rice during the cooking period breaks the coating of the rice releasing starch that sinks and sticks to the bottom of the sauce-pan causing the rice to burn.
This is also true when boiling peeled and sliced potatoes. There is less chance of the potatoes burning if you refrain from stirring.

BOILED BROWN RICE

2 cups long or short grain brown rice

❀ Place rice in a 2 or 3-quart saucepan. Rinse to get rid of any chaff and husks.

❀ Cover the surface of the rice with 1" of cold water.

❀ Cook uncovered, using high heat, till little craters begin to form on the surface of the rice and there is still a thin layer of water covering the surface. Do not stir and do not lower the heat during this cooking period. At this point, reduce heat to a simmer.

❀ Cover saucepan and simmer rice for 20 minutes. DO NOT peek during this simmering period. At the end of 20 minutes fluff rice and serve. If not serving at once, cover saucepan after fluffing and leave on warm range till ready to use.

Makes 6 cups

NOTE: Fingertip should be touching the SURFACE of the rice not through to the bottom of the saucepan.

ONE DISH CHICKEN & RICE

1½ cups basmati rice Rinse and drain using a strainer or a colander.
2 - 3 Chinese dried mushrooms Soak in ½ cup warm water to soften.
    Discard any stems. Dice or coarsely chop caps. Strain and reserve
    soaking liquid.
1½ cups chicken broth
2 tablespoons Szechuan preserved vegetables Chop coarsely.

*¾ pound lean chicken meat, leg
    or breast* Slice thinly.
1 tablespoon ginger wine, p.13
1 tablespoon regular soy sauce
1 tablespoon oyster sauce
½ teaspoon kosher salt or to taste
¼ teaspoon sugar
dash white pepper or to taste

Combine and marinate ½ hour at room temperature or overnight in the refrigerator.

1 cup frozen green peas Thaw and drain well.
½ cup diced red pepper
1 scallion Slice thinly.
¾ cup toasted cashew pieces

❀   Combine broth, mushroom liquid and additional water, if needed, to total 2 cups liquid.

❀   In a 3-quart saucepan, add rice, liquid, mushrooms and preserved vegetables. Bring to a boil, uncovered, using high heat. Stir in marinated chicken. Continue boiling, uncovered, till most of the liquid is absorbed. Cover saucepan. Reduce heat to a simmer or the lowest setting on your range and simmer 20 minutes. Stir in green peas, red pepper, scallion and cashews. Serve.

Serves 3 - 4

SESAME MUSHROOM RICE PILAF

1¼ cups long grain white rice Rinse and drain well. Place in a 3-quart saucepan.

4 - 6 Chinese dried mushrooms Soak in ½ cup warm water to soften. Discard any stems. Dice caps. Strain and reserve soaking liquid.

1 - 2 shallots, minced

1 clove garlic, minced

2 eggs, lightly beaten and scrambled

½ cup frozen peas Thaw and drain well.

½ cup coarsely chopped carrots

1 scallion, thinly sliced

1½ - 2 cups vegetable or chicken broth

2 teaspoons mushroom soy sauce

½ teaspoon oil

½ teaspoon sesame oil

white pepper to taste

1 - 3 teaspoons toasted sesame seeds (optional)

❀ Heat wok. Add oil, sesame oil, mushrooms, shallots and garlic. Stir-fry till mushrooms are fragrant. Add reserved mushroom liquid and soy sauce. Bring to a boil. Transfer to saucepan with rice.

❀ With your first finger touching the SURFACE of the rice, add broth to rice to reach the first joint of your finger.

❀ Cook uncovered, using high heat till most of the water has been absorbed and little craters begin to form on the surface of the rice. At this point, reduce hear to a simmer.

❀ Cover saucepan and simmer rice for 15 minutes. At the end of 15 minutes, fluff rice and stir in carrots. Cover and let stand on the warm range for 5 minutes.

❀ Stir in green peas, scallion, scrambled eggs and sesame seeds. Add white pepper to taste. Serve.

Serves 3 - 4

SHRIMP FRIED RICE

4 cups cooked white or brown rice
6 - 8 ounces shelled and deveined shrimp, diced

¼ teaspoon kosher salt
¼ teaspoon sugar
dash of white pepper
2 teaspoons ginger wine, p.13
a few slices ginger from ginger wine

Combine. Add shrimp and mix well.

2 eggs, lightly beaten
¾ cup frozen peas and carrots, thawed and drained well
1 scallion, thinly sliced
1 - 2 tablespoons dark soy sauce (optional)
1 teaspoon kosher salt or to taste
white pepper to taste
2 teaspoons oil
3 - 4 tablespoons broth or water

❀ Scramble eggs in a non-stick pan. Cut into small pieces.

❀ Heat wok. Add oil and shrimp. Stir-fry till shrimp changes color. Remove shrimp to a platter, leaving as much of the liquid in wok as possible.

❀ Add rice to wok. Stir-fry till the rice is heated through, adding broth 1 tablespoon at a time to prevent burning. Add soy sauce, 1 tablespoon at a time till desired color is reached.

❀ Add peas and carrots and scallion. Stir-fry till peas and carrots are heated through. Stir in scrambled eggs. Add salt and white pepper to taste. Serve.

Serves 3 - 4

VARIATIONS ON THE THEME

CHILI LOVERS: Add *Asian chili sauce* any time during cooking.

144   Rice

SHRIMP FRIED RICE (continued)

Do not limit yourself to frozen peas and carrots. Substitute or add the following, cut into small pieces, alone or in any combination: *asparagus, peppers, bean sprouts, blanched broccoli, cauliflower, green beans, bok choy, corn, chopped lettuce, or other seasonal vegetables.*

CURRY SHRIMP FRIED RICE

Add: *1 - 3 teaspoons curry powder or to taste.*
❀   Heat wok. Add oil and curry powder. Stir-fry 10 seconds. Add shrimp. Continue with the original recipe.

CHICKEN FRIED RICE

Substitute: *6 - 8 ounces coarsely chopped chicken breast* for the *shrimp.*

BEEF FRIED RICE

Substitute: *6 - 8 ounces coarsely chopped lean beef* for the *shrimp.*

VEGETARIAN FRIED RICE

Substitute: *4 ounces five-spiced pressed tofu* for the *shrimp.*
Cut tofu into small cubes, about the size of green peas.
❀   Skip the step for cooking shrimp.
❀   Heat wok. Add oil. Swirl to coat wok with oil. Add rice. Stir-fry till rice is heat through. Continue with the original recipe.
❀   Add tofu at the same time as peas and carrots.

ROAST PORK FRIED RICE

4 cups cooked white or brown rice
4 - 6 ounces Chinese roast pork (p.164), diced
2 eggs, lightly beaten
½ cup frozen peas and carrots, thawed and drained well
½ cup diced Chinese celery or regular celery
1 scallion, thinly sliced
2 - 4 tablespoons coarsely chopped Chinese parsley (optional)
1 - 2 tablespoons dark soy sauce
2 teaspoons kosher salt or to taste
white pepper to taste
2 teaspoons oil
3 - 4 tablespoons broth or water

❀   Scramble eggs in a non-stick pan. Cut into small pieces.

❀   Heat wok. Add oil, swirl to coat wok with oil. Add salt and rice to wok. Stir-fry till the rice is heated through, adding broth 1 tablespoon at a time to prevent burning. Add soy sauce 1 tablespoon at a time till desired color is reached.

❀   Add roast pork, peas and carrots, celery and scallion. Stir-fry till peas and carrots are heated through. Stir in scrambled eggs. Add salt and white pepper to taste. Transfer to a serving platter. Garnish with Chinese parsley. Serve.

Serves 3 - 4

VARIATIONS ON THE THEME

CHILI LOVERS: Add *Asian chili sauce* to taste any time.

Any kind of *cooked meat* can be substituted for the *Chinese roast pork.*

Chinese Noodles

151
Sesame Noodles
Sesame Noodles with Chicken

152
Chicken Lo Mein
Beef Lo Mein
Seafood Lo Mein

154
Roast Pork Lo Mein
Mushroom Lo Mein
Meatless Lo Mein

156
Hong Kong-style Noodles with Pacific Clams

157
Mee Fun with Dried Shrimp

158
Mee Fun with Chinese Ham & Dried Cranberries

159
Chicken Ho Fun

160
Curry Shrimp Ho Fun
Curry Fish Ho Fun

Noodle recipes in other sections of this book

MONEY-SAVING, TIME-SAVING TIPS

When boiling noodles or pasta, cook more than is needed for immediate use. Refrigerate the extra, making sure it is thoroughly cooled and well drained. It will keep for 3 - 4 days in the refrigerator, ready to be made into your favorite noodle salad or other noodle dishes.

Cook noodles and pasta in a large quantity of water. Bring water to a boil before adding noodles and pasta, and stir frequently during cooking.

To avoid boil-over and sticky pasta, always cook noodles and pasta uncovered. Should the water boil over, add ½ - 1 cup cold water to lower the water temperature.

Drain noodles or pasta as soon as it reaches the desired stage of doneness. If you are serving it immediately, there is no need to rinse. If it is to be held for later use, rinse under cold running water to stop any further cooking, and drain well.

ABOUT NOODLES

WHEAT NOODLES

There are a variety of noodles used in Chinese cuisine. The most common and widely used are egg noodles. These pale yellow noodles are made from wheat flour, egg, water and salt. They can be purchased in various thicknesses. The most common is the 1/16" cut (similar in size to number 8 spaghetti, which makes a good substitute). 1/16" egg noodles are referred to as lo mein noodles by some manufacturers. Another popular cut is about the thickness of thin spaghetti. This cut is often steamed and referred to as Hong Kong-style noodles. Then there are the ⅛" cut (similar to linguine) noodles, sometimes referred to as Cantonese noodles.

Another type of wheat noodle is made without egg. These off-white noodles are referred to as Shanghai noodles by some manufacturers,

WHEAT NOODLES (continued)

and also go by the name creamy Chinese-style noodles.

Wheat noodles can be purchased fresh (refrigerated), frozen or dried. I like to purchase my noodles fresh, repackage them in meal-sized portions and freeze for later use.

Store fresh noodles for up to 5 days in the refrigerator. Frozen noodles kept at 0°F or below keep up to 6 months. Dried noodles will keep indefinitely at room temperature in a dry area. Place dried noodles in a closed container with a few bay leaves to keep out bugs.

Any kind of pasta or egg noodle can be substituted for wheat noodles. Try substituting and experimenting with the various sizes and shapes available in the supermarket.

RICE NOODLES

Rice noodles are another widely used type of noodle. They are made from rice flour and water. Mee fun (rice sticks) are available in dried form and are sometimes referred to as rice vermicelli. These thin opaque noodles are somewhat brittle and turn white when soaked.

Ho fun is also made of rice. These noodles can be purchased fresh or dried. Fresh ho fun comes in a thin folded sheet weighing about 1 pound. Cut to desired width before using. Dried ho fun is precut in widths about ¼" thick and wider. Ho fun is really mee fun cut into wider ribbons.

Store fresh ho fun for up to 5 days in the refrigerator. Dried ho fun and mee fun will keep indefinitely at room temperature. There is no substitute for rice noodles.

BEAN NOODLES

Then there are bean noodles, made from mung bean flour and water. These noodles are available in two forms. Fun sze (bean thread) are

BEAN NOODLES (continued)

thin, semi-transparent and wiry noodles, also referred to as glass noodles or cellophane noodles. Bean thread can be purchased in a variety of package sizes, ranging from 1.7 ounces to 1 pound.

It is easier to cut bean thread after it has soaked in warm water for about 15 minutes. If you must cut bean thread in its dry form, be prepared for the strands to fly in all directions. To make the job easier and less messy, put bean thread in a large plastic or paper bag and cut with a pair of strong scissors.

The other form of bean noodle is a thin, circular translucent sheet that look likes a piece of plastic. This is called Tianjin fun pi (Tianjin green bean starch sheet). Soak in warm water for about 15 minutes to soften, then cut to desired size.

Bean noodles are usually served as part of a meal and eaten with rice, never alone. Because of their highly absorbent quality, bean noodles are frequently paired with vegetables that have a high water content, such as napa cabbage, bok choy and fuzzy melon. Bean noodles are also frequently added to soup and stew to give texture and substance.

Bean noodles will keep indefinitely at room temperature. There is no substitute for bean noodles.

SESAME NOODLES

1 pound fresh Chinese egg noodles Cut to desired length.
2 teaspoons Asian sesame oil
4 ounces snow peas Remove ends and strings. Shred.
1 carrots, shredded
8 ounces bean sprouts Parboil 10 seconds. Drain and pat dry.
1 scallion Slant-cut into thin slices.
2 tablespoons coarsely chopped unsalted roasted peanuts

4 tablespoons toasted sesame seeds Ground to a paste (see note). *1 - 2 tablespoons rice vinegar* *4 tablespoons regular soy sauce* *1 teaspoon sugar* *1 - 3 teaspoons Asian chili sauce* *1 - 2 cloves garlic,* puréed *¼ - ½ teaspoon white pepper*	Combine in a bowl. Mix to dissolve sugar and blend in sesame seed paste, adding broth or water as needed to reach a consistency of heavy cream. This is the dressing.

❀   Parboil noodles in a large pot of boiling water till just done (about 6 minutes). Drain well immediately. Transfer cooked noodles onto a large baking pan or a cookie sheet.

❀   Add sesame oil. Toss to evenly coat the noodles with the sesame oil. Spread out to cool, tossing every now and then till completely cooled. Toss with sesame seed dressing to taste.

❀   Add snow peas, carrots bean sprouts and scallion. Mix well. Arrange on serving platter. Sprinkle peanuts on top and serve.

Serves 4 - 5

NOTE: You may substitute 2 - 3 tablespoons store-bought Asian sesame seed paste.

VARIATION ON THE THEME

SESAME NOODLES WITH CHICKEN

Add: *1 whole poached or baked chicken breast* Shred along the grain.

CHICKEN LO MEIN

1 pound fresh Chinese egg noodles Cut to desired length.

½ - 1 pound chicken breasts, thinly sliced
1 teaspoon kosher salt or to taste
1 teaspoon sugar
1 teaspoon dark soy sauce
2 teaspoons regular soy sauce
1 tablespoon ginger wine, p.13
white pepper to taste

Combine. Marinate ½ hour at room tempera ture. Chicken can be marinated the day be fore and refrigerated.

½ - 1 pound green cabbage Cut into ½" wide strips
2 ounces snow peas Remove ends and strings
2 - 3 ribs celery Slant-cut into ½" wide pieces.
1 - 2 carrots Slant-cut into thin slices.
½ cup chicken broth
½ - 1 teaspoon kosher salt or to taste
1 teaspoon oil
1 clove garlic, minced
1 shallot, minced
1 - 2 tablespoons oyster sauce or mushroom soy sauce

2 teaspoons cornstarch
1 tablespoon water

Combine in a small dish. Stir before adding to wok.

❀   Bring a large pot of water to a boil. Add noodles and cook, uncovered, till al dente, about 6 minutes. Drain.

❀   While water is boiling, bring 2 tablespoons broth to a boil in a wok, using high heat. Add salt and vegetables. Stir-fry till vegetables are slightly under desired doneness, adding broth 1 tablespoon at a time to prevent burning. Remove vegetables and any remaining broth to a platter.

❀   Heat wok. Add oil, garlic and shallot. Stir-fry, using medium heat, till garlic is lightly browned. Add chicken, stir-fry, using high

Chicken Lo Mein (continued)

heat, till chicken changes color, adding broth 1 tablespoon at a time to prevent burning. Add remaining broth. Bring to a boil. Boil 1 - 2 minutes or till chicken is cooked. Thicken with cornstarch mixture.

✿ Add drained noodles. Stir-fry till noodles are evenly coated with sauce and heated through. Stir in oyster sauce to taste.

✿ Add vegetables. Mix well. Add salt to taste. Serve.

Serves 4 - 5

Variations on the Theme

CHILI LOVERS: Add *Asian chili sauce* any time during cooking.

Do not limit yourself to the vegetables mentioned in the recipe. Substitute or add, alone or in combination: *asparagus, bok choy, napa cabbage, green beans, bean sprouts, blanched broccoli, cauliflower, gai lan, choy sum, red peppers, green peppers, lettuce, or other seasonal vegetables.*

Beef Lo Mein

Substitute: *½ - 1 pound lean beef* for the *chicken.*
Add: *1 - 2 teaspoons cornstarch* to the marinade.
Eliminate: *2 teaspoons cornstarch* and *1 tablespoon water.*

Seafood Lo Mein

Substitute: *4 - 8 ounces shelled shrimp* and *4 - 8 ounces scallops* for the *chicken.*

ROAST PORK LO MEIN

1 pound fresh Chinese egg noodles Cut to desired length.
4 - 8 ounces Chinese roast pork, thinly sliced or shredded, p.164
½ - 1 pound bite-sized, blanched broccoli florets
1 onion Cut into 6 - 8 lengthwise wedges.
2 - 4 ounces mushrooms, sliced
2 - 3 ribs celery Slant-cut into ½" wide pieces.
1 - 2 carrots Slant-cut into thin slices.
½ cup chicken broth
1 teaspoon oil
1 clove garlic, minced
1 shallot, minced
1 teaspoon kosher salt or to taste
1 teaspoon sugar
white pepper to taste
1 tablespoon ginger wine, p.13
1 tablespoon regular soy sauce
1 tablespoon oyster sauce or mushroom soy sauce

2 teaspoons cornstarch ⎤ Combine in a small dish. Stir
1 tablespoon water   ⎦ before adding to wok.

❀ Bring a large pot of water to a boil. Add noodles and cook, uncovered, till al dente, about 6 minutes. Drain.

❀ While water is boiling, bring 2 tablespoons broth to a boil in a wok, using high heat. Add salt and vegetables. Stir-fry till vegetables are slightly under desired doneness, adding broth 1 tablespoon at a time to prevent burning. Remove vegetables and any remaining broth to a platter.

❀ Heat wok. Add oil, garlic and shallot. Stir-fry, using medium heat, till garlic is lightly browned. Add remaining broth, roast pork, sugar, white pepper, ginger wine, regular soy sauce and oyster sauce. Bring to a boil, using high heat.

ROAST PORK LO MEIN (continued)

❀   Thicken with cornstarch mixture. Add drained noodles. Stir-fry till noodles are evenly coated with sauce and heated through.

❀   Add vegetables. Mix well. Add salt to taste. Serve.

Serves 4 - 5

VARIATIONS ON THE THEME

CHILI LOVERS: Add *Asian chili sauce* any time during cooking.

Any kind of cooked meat can be substituted for the roast pork. This is a great recipe to use up some of the leftover Thanksgiving turkey and Easter ham or to stretch a few slices of leftover roast beef or chicken.

MUSHROOM LO MEIN

Substitute: *1 - 3 ounces Chinese dried mushrooms* for the *roast pork.* Soak mushrooms in warm water for 30 minutes to soften. Remove and discard any stems. Shred caps.

❀   Add mushrooms to oil at the same time as garlic. Stir-fry till mushrooms are fragrant.

MEATLESS LO MEIN

Substitute: *4 - 8 ounces five-spice pressed tofu* for the *roast pork.*

HONG KONG-STYLE NOODLES WITH PACIFIC CLAMS

1 pound Hong Kong-style noodles
1 15-ounce can Pacific clams Drain, reserving liquid.
1 can baby corn, drained and rinsed
½ can straw mushrooms, drained and rinsed
2 - 4 ounces snow peas Remove ends and strings.
1 large onion Cut into 6 - 8 lengthwise wedges.
a few slices carrots or a few strips red pepper
2 scallions, cut into 1" lengths
1 - 2 cloves garlic, minced
1 teaspoon kosher salt or to taste
¼ teaspoon white pepper or to taste
1 teaspoon oil

¼ cup chicken broth
2 tablespoons ginger wine, p.13
1 - 2 tablespoons oyster sauce
*   or mushroom soy sauce*
1 teaspoon sugar
2 teaspoons cornstarch

Combine in a small bowl. Stir well just before adding to wok. This is the sauce.

❀ Bring a large pot of water to a boil. Add noodles and cook uncovered for 1 minute. Drain.

❀ While water is boiling, heat wok. Add oil, scallions and garlic. Stir-fry, using medium heat, till garlic is lightly browned. Add vegetables, salt and white pepper. Stir-fry, using high heat, till snow peas change color.

❀ Add clam liquid and sauce. Bring to a boil, stirring constantly. Boil 1 minute. Add clams, mix well.

❀ Add drained noodles. Mix well. Serve.

Serves 4 - 5

MEE FUN WITH DRIED SHRIMP

½ pound mee fun Rinse. Soak in warm water for 5 minutes to soften.
1 - 3 ounces small dried shrimp Rinse. Soak in ¼ cup warm water for
    at least 15 minutes.
2 - 3 Chinese dried mushrooms Soak in warm water for 30 minutes.
    Remove and discard any stems. Shred caps.
½ cup shredded red pepper
1 pound bean sprouts
½ - 1 cup 1" lengths Chinese chives or shredded scallions
2 cooked scrambled eggs Coarsely chop.
1 teaspoon oil
1 teaspoon kosher salt

1 cup chicken broth
1 tablespoon oyster sauce
    or mushroom soy sauce   Combine in a small bowl.
2 tablespoons ginger wine, p.13   This the sauce.
½ teaspoon white pepper or to taste
Asian chili sauce to taste (optional)

❀   Drain shrimp. Strain and reserve liquid.

❀   In a wok or frying pan, bring 2 tablespoons broth or water to a
boil, using high heat. Add salt, red pepper, bean sprouts and Chinese
chives. Stir-fry till bean sprouts lose their raw taste, about 1- 2
minutes. Remove vegetables and any remaining liquid to a platter.

❀   Heat wok. Add oil, drained shrimp and mushrooms. Stir-fry, using
medium-high heat, till mushrooms are fragrant, adding reserved shrimp
liquid 1 tablespoon at a time to prevent burning.

❀   Add mee fun and ¼ cup sauce. Stir-fry, using medium to medium-
high heat. Continue stir-frying and adding sauce till all the sauce is
used and mee fun is soft. Mix in vegetables and scrambled eggs. Add
salt to taste. Serve.

Serves 3 - 4

Mee Fun with Chinese Ham & Dried Cranberries

½ pound mee fun Rinse. Soak in warm water for 5 minutes to soften.
2 ounces Chinese ham or other dry-cured ham, coarsely chopped
2 - 3 Chinese dried mushrooms Soak in warm water for 30 minutes.
    Remove and discard any stems. Coarsely chop or shred caps.
1 carrot, shredded
½ pound zucchini, shredded
½ pound yellow squash, shredded
½ - 1 cup 1" lengths Chinese chives or shredded scallions
2 - 3 tablespoons dried cranberries
1 teaspoon oil
1 - 2 cloves garlic, minced
1 teaspoon kosher salt

1 cup chicken broth
1 tablespoon mushroom soy sauce   Combine in a small bowl.
2 tablespoons ginger wine, p.13   This the sauce.
½ teaspoon white pepper or to taste

❀   In a wok or frying pan, bring 2 tablespoons broth or water to a boil, using high heat. Add salt, carrot, zucchini, yellow squash and chives. Stir-fry till vegetables are slightly under desired doneness. Remove vegetables and any remaining liquid to a platter.

❀   Heat wok, all oil, garlic and mushrooms. Stir-fry, using medium-high heat, till mushrooms are fragrant, adding sauce 1 tablespoon at a time to prevent burning.

❀   Add mee fun and ¼ cup sauce. Stir-fry, using medium to medium high heat. Continue stir-frying and adding sauce till all the sauce is used and mee fun is soft. Mix in vegetables, ham and cranberries. Add salt to taste. Serve.

Serves 3 - 4

Chicken Ho Fun

1 - 2 pounds fresh ho fun Cut into ½" wide strips. Microwave 2 - 6 minutes or till heated through.

½ pound chicken breasts, thinly sliced
1 tablespoon ginger wine, p.13
1 teaspoon cornstarch
2 teaspoons dark soy sauce
1 teaspoon regular soy sauce
½ teaspoon kosher salt or to taste
½ teaspoon sugar or to taste
white pepper to taste

Combine. Marinate ½ hour at room temperature or overnight in the refrigerator.

½ pound napa cabbage Cut into ½" wide strips.
½ pound asparagus Peel. Cut into 1" lengths.
few strips yellow pepper
few strips red pepper
1 scallion Cut into 1" lengths.
2 - 4 tablespoons chicken broth
1 teaspoon kosher salt or to taste

❀ In a wok or large frying pan, bring 2 tablespoons broth to a boil using high heat. Add salt and vegetables. Stir-fry till vegetables are slightly under desired doneness. Remove all the vegetables to a plate, leaving as much of the liquid as possible in the wok.

❀ Return liquid in wok to a boil. Add chicken, stir-fry till chicken is cooked, adding broth as needed to prevent burning.

❀ Add vegetables and ho fun. Mix well. Add salt to taste. Serve.

Serves 3 - 4

CURRY SHRIMP HO FUN

1 - 2 pound fresh ho fun Cut into ½" wide strips. Microwave 2- 6
    minutes or till heated through.
½ pound large raw shrimp Shell, devein, rinse and pat dry.
1 teaspoons oil
1 - 3 tablespoons curry powder or to taste
¼ - 2 teaspoons Asian chili sauce
1 teaspoon kosher salt or to taste
1 tablespoon minced shallots
2 - 3 cloves garlic, minced
1 - 2 tomatoes Peel. Discard seeds. Chop coarsely.
1 onion Peel. Cut into ¾" chunks.
¾ - 1 cup broth
2 - 3 tablespoons coarsely chopped Chinese parsley

❉ Heat wok. Add oil and curry powder. Stir-fry about 5 seconds, using medium heat. Add chili sauce, salt, shallots and garlic. Stir-fry about 2 minutes or till shallots and garlic are translucent, adding broth 1 tablespoon at a time to prevent burning.

❉ Add shrimp and tomatoes. Stir-fry till shrimp changes color and is well coated with curry mixture. Add what remains of the ¾ cup of broth. Bring to a boil. Simmer 5 minutes or till shrimp is cooked, adding more broth to make the finished dish the consistency of a stew.

❉ Divide hot ho fun among 4 soup plates or large soup bowls. Spoon shrimp mixture on top, garnish with Chinese parsley and serve.

Serves 4

VARIATION ON THE THEME

Curry Fish Ho Fun

Substitute: *¾ pound cod, haddock or red snapper* for the *shrimp*
    Cut fish into bite-sized pieces.

THE COCKTAIL HOUR

163
Scallop & Papaya Salad
*Macaroni Salad with
Scallops & Papaya*

164
**Chinese Roast Pork with
Maple Syrup**
*Chinese Roast Pork on a Pick
Maple Syrup Pork Chops
Barbecued Maple Syrup Chicken*

166
**Tea-smoked Salmon In
a Wok**
Tea Smoked Shrimp In a Wok

167
Shrimp Toast

168
Grilled Plum Wine Shrimp
*Grilled Plum Wine Shrimp with
Baby Squash
Grilled Plum Wine Chicken
Grilled Plum Wine Beef with
Peppers*

170
Beef & Scallion Rolls
*Beef & Vegetable Rolls
Turkey Logs on a Stick
Sesame Beef & Scallion Rolls*

172
**Five-spice Pressed Tofu
with Peanut Sauce**

MONEY-SAVING, TIME-SAVING TIPS

Most of the recipes in this section can also be served as main dishes. Similarly, many recipes in the other sections can be used as appetizers or for cocktail parties.

Most of the recipes can be prepared ahead of time. Many of the dishes can be frozen and reheated at the last minute; others refrigerated with minimum effort before serving.

If you want to entertain but do not wish to have a formal seated dinner, why not have a Chinese cocktail party? Serve bite-sized items that do not require diners to fuss with knives and forks. Everyone is free to walk around and mingle at an informal yet elegant Chinese cocktail party.

SCALLOP & PAPAYA SALAD

1 pound bay scallops
4 cups dry white wine
thumb-size piece of ginger Peel and smash.
2 - 4 plum tomatoes Seed and cut into ½" cubes.
½ - 1 papaya Peel and seed. Cut into ½" cubes.
½ - 1 red onion, coarsely chopped
¼ - ½ cup coarsely chopped Chinese parsley or to taste
1 tablespoon finely shredded fresh ginger or to taste
2 - 4 tablespoons rice vinegar or to taste
sugar to taste
kosher salt to taste
white pepper to taste

❀ In a 3 or 4-quart saucepan, bring white wine to a boil, using medium heat. Add scallops. Bring to a boil. Reduce heat to medium-low and simmer 3 minutes or till scallops are opaque and firm. Drain scallops well. Spread on a large platter to cool. Discard cooking liquid.

❀ Combine cooled scallops with remaining ingredients. Marinate at least 1 hour in the refrigerator. Serve.

SERVING SUGGESTIONS: Serve with toasted or untoasted pita wedges, crackers or Melba toast.

VARIATION ON THE THEME

MACARONI SALAD WITH SCALLOPS & PAPAYA

Add: *4 - 8 ounces of cooked macaroni*
    1 - 2 tablespoons dried blueberries.

CHINESE ROAST PORK WITH MAPLE SYRUP

3 pounds lean pork shoulder or pork sirloin Remove and discard all visible fat. Cut into long strips about ¾" wide and ¾" thick. Using a fork or a small sharp knife, pierce pork strips at about 1½" intervals. This will result in more evenly marinated roast pork.

½ teaspoon five-spice powder
½ teaspoon kosher salt or to taste
¼ cup maple syrup or to taste
1 tablespoon brown sugar
2 tablespoons ginger wine, p.13
1 tablespoon oyster sauce
1 tablespoon dark soy sauce
1 tablespoon regular soy sauce
1 tablespoons hoisin sauce
1 square (about 1 tablespoon) red bean curd
3 - 4 cloves garlic

Purée, using a hand blender or a food processor. Add pork strips. Mix to coat each strip well with marinade. Marinate at least 2 hours, or preferably overnight, in the refrigerator, turning once or twice. For a more pronounced flavor, marinate up to 2 days in the refrigerator.

❀   Preheat broiler. Pour 1 cup warm water in the broiler pan. Place broiler rack on top. Brush rack with lemon juice.

❀   Remove pork strips from marinade and arrange in one layer on broiler rack, leaving space between strips. Broil on high, in the middle of the oven, for 6 minutes. Turn each strip.

❀   Broil on high another 6 - 8 minutes or till pork is cooked.

❀   Cut into thin slices or cubes. Serve warm or at room temperature.

NOTE: Chinese Roast Pork freezes well. Make extra for the freezer. It's a great item to have on hand because of its versatility and ease of use. You can make Roast Pork Fried Rice, p.146 or Roast Pork Lo Mein, p.154. For a fast meal, stir-fry available vegetables to desired doneness, toss in some sliced roast pork and serve with rice—a complete meal in under 30 minutes, start to finish.

Variations on the Theme

Chinese Roast Pork on a Pick

Add individually or in any combination: *red cherry tomatoes, yellow cherry tomatoes, green grapes, melon balls, strawberries, pineapple chunks, cubes of grilled summer squash, chunks of kiwi, or other fruits or cooked vegetables.*

❀ Cut roast pork into ¾" cubes. Thread on a toothpick.

❀ Top with any of the above fruits and vegetables.

Maple Syrup Pork Chops

Substitute: *Pork chops* for the *pork shoulder.*
                Leave pork chops whole.

Barbecued Maple Syrup Chicken

Substitute: *Chicken legs* for the *pork*
                1 tablespoon bean sauce for the *red bean curd.*
Add: *¼ - 2 teaspoons Asian chili sauce* to the marinade.

❀ Grill or bake 35 - 45 minutes or till cooked through. Remove and discard skin before serving.

TEA-SMOKED SALMON IN A WOK

1 pound salmon fillets ⎤ Cut fillets into ¾" wide strips. Sprinkle
2 - 3 teaspoons kosher salt ⎥ on salt and sugar. Mix well. Refrigerate
2 teaspoons brown sugar ⎦ at least 2 hours, preferably overnight.

2 tablespoons lichee black tea leaves
2 tablespoons dark brown sugar
a few thin strips of dried tangerine peel (optional)
honeydew melon chunks or wedges

❊ Line a 14" round-bottomed wok with heavy duty aluminum foil, allowing foil to extend at least 2" past the edge of the wok.

❊ Sprinkle tea leaves, sugar and tangerine peel on top of foil. Place a round 9"-10" rack in wok. Arrange salmon strips on rack, leaving space between strips.

❊ Line wok cover with heavy duty aluminum foil, allowing foil to extend at least 2" past the edge of the cover. Cover wok. Crimp the foil from the wok and its cover tightly together.

❊ Place wok on range. Smoke on high for 5 minutes. Lower range setting to medium-high. Smoke another 5 minutes. Turn off heat. Let wok sit on warm range for 3 - 4 minutes (see note). Serve warm or at room temperature with honeydew melon.

Serves 3 - 4

NOTE: This is a high-salt dish. Balance it with low-salt grain dishes and low-salt vegetable dishes.
The smoking time given is for salmon at refrigerator temperature. You may need to adjust the time if salmon is at room temperature.

VARIATION ON THE THEME

TEA-SMOKED SHRIMP IN A WOK

Substitute: *1½ pounds raw shrimp* for the *salmon*.
❊ Smoke shrimp shelled or unshelled.

SHRIMP TOAST

½ *pound shrimp* Shell, devein,
    rinse and pat dry well.
1 teaspoon kosher salt

Combine. Let marinate 15 minutes.

1 egg white, lightly beaten
2 tablespoons minced water chestnuts
1 tablespoon ginger wine, p.13
½ - 1 teaspoon sesame oil
pinch of sugar
white pepper to taste
Asian chili sauce to taste
2 teaspoons chopped Chinese chives or scallions
2 teaspoons coarsely chopped Chinese parsley
¼ cup mashed potatoes
20 - 24 melba toast rounds
1 - 2 teaspoons toasted black sesame seeds

❀   Mince shrimp by hand or pulse for a few seconds in the food processor. Do not purée. Transfer minced shrimp to mixing bowl.

❀   Add egg white, water chestnuts, ginger wine, sesame oil, sugar, white pepper, chili sauce, Chinese chives, Chinese parsley and mashed potatoes to minced shrimp. Combine well.

❀   Spread Melba toast rounds with shrimp mixture. Sprinkle a few sesame seeds on top, pressing lightly to make sure seeds adhere. Place on ungreased baking pan or cookie sheet.

❀   Broil on high, in the middle of the oven, for 4 - 7 minutes or till lightly browned. Serve at once.

Makes 20 - 24 appetizers

GRILLED PLUM WINE SHRIMP

1 pound large shrimp Peel, devein, wash and pat dry well.
1 teaspoon kosher salt

⎫ Combine. Marinate 15 minutes.

2 tablespoons plum wine
1 tablespoon lime juice
1 teaspoon grated fresh ginger or to taste
1 clove garlic, pureed
2 - 3 scallions, smashed

⎫ Combine in a large non reactive bowl. This is the marinade.

wedges of black and green plums for garnish or as an accompaniment
10 - 12 10" bamboo skewers Soak in water at least 30 minutes to prevent burning.

❋ Combine shrimp and marinade. Marinate 15 minutes.

❋ Drain shrimp. Thread 3 - 4 shrimp onto each bamboo skewer. Grill (or broil on high in the middle of the oven) 5 - 8 minutes or till done, turning once. Serve hot or at room temperature.

Makes 10 - 12 kabobs

VARIATIONS ON THE THEME

CHILI LOVERS: Add *Asian chili sauce* to taste to marinade.

GRILLED PLUM WINE SHRIMP WITH BABY SQUASH

Add: *baby pattypan squash, yellow squash* and *baby zucchini.* Cut squash into 1" chunks.
❋ Alternate shrimp and squash on bamboo skewers.

GRILLED PLUM WINE SHRIMP (continued)

GRILLED PLUM WINE CHICKEN

Substitute: *¾ pound chicken breasts* for the *shrimp*.
        Slice chicken into long thin strips.
Eliminate: *1 teaspoon kosher salt.*
Add: *1 tablespoon regular soy sauce* to the marinade.
❀   Thread chicken strips accordion style onto the bamboo skewers.
Grill or broil 6 - 8 minutes or till done, turning occasionally.

GRILLED PLUM WINE BEEF WITH PEPPERS

Substitute: *¾ pound lean sirloin steak* for the *shrimp*.
        Cut beef into ¾" cubes.
Eliminate: *1 teaspoon kosher salt.*
Add: *1 tablespoon oyster sauce* or *1 tablespoon mushroom soy sauce*
    to the marinade
    1 - 2 chopped fresh red or green chili peppers to the marinade
    ½ - 1 each green, red and orange sweet peppers
    Cut sweet peppers into 1" squares.
❀   Alternate beef cubes and pepper squares onto bamboo skewers.
Grill or broil 8 - 10 minutes or till done, turning occasionally.

BEEF & SCALLION ROLLS

1 pound lean sirloin steak Remove and discard all visible fat. Slice across the grain into long thin strips.

1 tablespoon brown sugar
2 tablespoons ginger wine, p.13
1 tablespoon mushroom or dark soy sauce — Combine well. Add
1 - 2 tablespoons hoisin sauce — sliced beef. Mix to coat
1 teaspoon cornstarch — each strip. This can be
½ teaspoon kosher salt or to taste — done the day before and
1 teaspoon puréed garlic or to taste — refrigerated.

3 - 4 scallions Cut into 2" lengths.
20 - 25 round toothpicks Soak in water 30 minutes to prevent burning.

2 tablespoons honey
1 tablespoon warm water — Combine in a small dish.

❈ Roll 2 or 3 lengths of scallion in one strip of beef. Fasten with a toothpick. Place on a baking pan brushed with lemon juice or a non-stick baking pan. Repeat with remaining scallion and beef. Brush rolls with honey mixture.

❈ Bake at 400°F, in the middle of the oven for 9 - 12 minutes or till done, turning once. Serve hot or at room temperature.

Makes 20 - 25 rolls

VARIATIONS ON THE THEME

CHILI LOVERS: Add *Asian chili sauce* to taste to marinade.

BEEF & SCALLION ROLLS (continued)

BEEF & VEGETABLE ROLLS

Substitute: *asparagus tips, sugar snap peas, green beans, broccoli florets, carrot sticks, sweet pepper sticks, or whole fresh chilies* for the *scallions*.

❀   Blanch asparagus tips and sugar snap peas in boiling water for 10 seconds. Drain and cool under cold running water. Drain again.

❀   Blanch green beans, broccoli florets and carrots sticks in boiling water for 1 minute. Drain and cool under cold running water. Drain.

TURKEY LOGS ON A STICK

Substitute: *1 pound turkey breast* for the *beef.*

Cut turkey breast into 3" × ½" × ½" logs.

Eliminate: *scallions.*

Substitute: *10" bamboo skewers* for the *toothpicks.*

Soak bamboo skewers in water for 30 minutes before using to prevent burning.

❀   Push bamboo skewers through the middle (lengthwise) of turkey logs.

SESAME BEEF & SCALLION ROLLS

Add: *1 teaspoon Asian chili sauce or to taste* to the marinade.

1 - 2 tablespoon toasted sesame seeds and *1 teaspoon sesame oil* to the marinade.

Crush sesame seeds, leaving some of the seeds whole, before adding to the marinade.

FIVE-SPICE PRESSED TOFU KABOBS WITH PEANUT SAUCE

8 - 12 ounces five-spice pressed tofu Cut into ¾" cubes.

1 can baby corn Drain and cut each ear into 2 or 3 sections.

2 - 4 ounces snow peas Remove ends and strings. Blanch in boiling water for 10 seconds. Cool under cold running water. Drain. Cut each snow pea into 3 - 4 sections.

½ - 1 red pepper Cut into ¾" squares.

4" frilled toothpicks

2 tablespoons smooth peanut butter *1 tablespoon lime juice* *1 tablespoon rice vinegar* *3 tablespoons regular soy sauce* *1 - 2 teaspoons sugar or to taste* *1 - 3 teaspoons Asian chili sauce* *1 - 2 cloves garlic,* puréed *1 - 2 tablespoons coarsely chopped* *Chinese parsley*	Combine in a small bowl. Add water 1 tablespoon at a time to reach a consistency of heavy cream. This is the peanut sauce.

❀ Thread tofu on toothpicks, alternating with vegetables. Arrange on serving platter with peanut sauce on the side.

CHA (TEA)
The national drink of the Chinese

176
Iced Lichee Tea with Chinese Rock Sugar

CHA (TEA)

Chinese teas are divided into three main categories: green teas, black teas (the English translation for the Chinese characters meaning "red tea") and oolong teas.

Green teas are unfermented teas. The dried leaves retain their green color. When brewing green tea, bring clean fresh water to a boil. Allow to cool about 1 minute, then pour over tea leaves. Cover and let stand about 3 minutes. You will have to experiment to find the correct water temperature and amount of tea leaves to suit your individual taste. If the water is too hot, brewed green tea will have a slightly bitter taste; if it is not hot enough, the tea will lack flavor. Brewed green tea has a light color and a clean, delicate taste. Do not judge the strength of brewed green tea by its color. Lung-ching cha (dragon's well tea) and gunpowder tea are two of the most popular green teas.

Black teas are fully fermented teas. The resulting beverage is full-bodied and strong-tasting. Brew black teas using boiling water. Keemun black tea is one of the best known.

Oolong teas are semi-fermented teas. This class of tea possesses a wide range of color, taste and aroma that falls between green teas and black teas, depending on what stage the fermentation process was halted at. A short fermentation period will result in a tea with color and character closer to that of green tea. A longer fermentation period will produce a darker and more robust tea. Brew oolong teas using boiling water or slightly cooled boiled water. This again requires some experimentation to accommodate your individual taste and the type of oolong tea. Some of the more well known oolong teas are ti kuan yin (iron goddess of mercy) and suei shen (water fairy).

There are also a number of teas scented with flowers or flavored with dried fruits. Scented teas include jasmine, rose and chrysanthemum. The most popular fruit-flavored tea is lichee black tea. There are also tea flavored with strawberries, persimmon, mango and ginger.

CHA (TEA) (continued)

These flavored teas make excellent iced tea.

Tea is a stimulant and does contain caffeine. Black tea has a higher caffeine content than green tea. The caffeine content of tea, however, is lower than the caffeine content of coffee.

The general guidelines for brewing tea are:

❀ *Use fresh cold water.*

❀ *Use 1 teaspoon of tea leaves for every cup of water.* This is just a guideline; adjust to individual preferences as necessary. Brewing time will vary also depending on the type of leaves. Use 3 minutes as a guide and adjust accordingly.

❀ *Pour boiling water onto tea leaves.* To avoid flat-tasting tea, pour water onto tea leaves as soon as it comes to a boil. Boiling the water for too long will boil away the oxygen in the water, resulting in flat-tasting tea.

When using an infuser or tea ball, allow room for leaves to expand while steeping.

There are many grades of tea and the prices will vary greatly. Generally, the higher the price, the better the quality.

Store teas in an odor-free, airtight container in a cool, dry place out of direct sunlight.

ICED LICHEE TEA WITH CHINESE ROCK SUGAR

¼ cup loose lichee black tea leaves
2 - 3 tablespoons pulverized Chinese rock sugar or
*   white sugar to taste*
12 cups freshly drawn cold water
fresh mint sprigs for garnish

❀   In a non-aluminum pot, bring water to a boil. Add tea leaves. Cover and remove from heat. Steep 3 minutes.

❀   Stir. Strain into a pitcher. Sweeten to taste. Cool.

❀   Use some of the cooled tea to make tea ice cubes. Refrigerate the remainder.

❀   To serve: Place a couple of tea ice cubes in a glass, pour tea over, garnish with a sprig of mint and enjoy.

Makes about 3 quarts

VARIATIONS ON THE THEME

❀   Reduce sugar and add juice from canned lichees.

❀   Substitute other fruit-flavored or scented teas for the lichee tea.

❀   Substitute honey for the sugar.

DESSERT

179
Persimmon Fan with Blueberries & Ice Cream

180
Berries Parfait
Papaya Parfait

181
Papaya Fruit Cup

182
Berries in Plum Wine
Citrus Fruits in Plum Wine
Plums in Plum Wine
Melons in Plum Wine

183
Tropical Fruit Cup

184
Minted Melon Balls
Minted Melon Balls with Lichees

185
Persimmon Sherbet

185
Autumn Fruits with Honey & Lime

MONEY-SAVING, TIME-SAVING TIPS

With the exception of special occasions, like birthdays and weddings, Chinese people do not typically end a meal with cake or pastries. Instead dessert is usually seasonal fresh fruit.

By using seasonal fresh fruit, you are not only getting fruits at their best quality but also at their best price. Buying fruits in season also assures you of a wider selection.

If you live near or have the opportunity to visit a fruit farm, you may like to consider canning, freezing or drying sun-ripened seasonal fruits for out-of-season use.

Persimmons (both the Hachiya and the Fuyu freeze well) and blueberries are two of the easiest fruits to freeze: Wash, drain, place in freezer bag or container. Label, date and freeze. These fruit will keep for up to 3 months. Nothing could be easier.

PERSIMMON FAN WITH BLUEBERRIES & ICE CREAM

(This recipe requires advance preparation)

2 frozen Hachiya persimmons (see note)
½ cup fresh blueberries
4 scoops vanilla ice cream or vanilla frozen yogurt
4 sprigs of fresh mint

❀   Prepare 4 dessert plates for use.

❀   Remove and discard persimmon caps. Peel persimmons. Cut in half lengthwise. Cut each half into 4 or 5 lengthwise wedges. Fan out wedges and place on a dessert plate. Repeat with the other four halves. (Persimmons can be prepared ahead of time, wrapped in freezer wrap and frozen. Place in the refrigerator 1 hour before serving to thaw.)

❀   Put 1 scoop of ice cream at the base of each persimmon fan. Sprinkle with 2 tablespoons blueberries. Garnish with a sprig of fresh mint.

Serves 4

NOTE: Wash and dry fresh persimmons. Place in a freezer bag and freeze. Frozen persimmons will keep up to 3 months.
There are two kinds of persimmons—Hachiya and Fuyu—available in Asian stores and supermarkets.
The Hachiya persimmon is a large, acorn-shaped fruit. The ripened fruit is soft and very sweet. Choose fruits that are a deep rich orange color and are soft with smooth, unblemished skin. If not quite ripe when purchased, leave at room temperature to ripen.
The Fuyu persimmon is a smaller, rounded fruit and lighter in color than the Hachiya. The ripened fruit remains firm, crisp and very sweet. Choose fruit with smooth unblemished skin.

BERRIES PARFAIT

1 cup fresh blackberries
1 cup fresh red raspberries
1 cup fresh blueberries
4 large strawberries with caps
½ pint vanilla ice cream or vanilla frozen yogurt
4 sprigs of fresh mint

❀ Prepare 4 parfait glasses or any tall glasses for use.

❀ Slice each strawberry lengthwise, from the pointed end three-quarters of the way to the cap. Do not remove caps. Fan out the slices.

❀ Place 2 tablespoons ice cream at the bottom of a glass. Top with 2 tablespoons blackberries. Repeat procedure with ice cream and raspberries, and ice cream and blueberries. Ending with a layer of ice cream. Top with a strawberry fan and a sprig of mint.

❀ Repeat with other glasses.

Serves 4

VARIATION ON THE THEME

PAPAYA PARFAIT

Substitute: *orange and yellow papayas* for the *berries.*
        Peel papayas. Remove and discard seeds. Cut into small
        chunks.
Add: *1 - 2 tablespoons toasted sliced almonds.*
❀ Sprinkle toasted almonds on top and serve.

Papaya Fruit Cup

2 papayas (see note)
1 15-ounce can longans Drain and reserve liquid.
2 kiwis Peel and cut into small chunks.
1 cup fresh red raspberries
1 cup fresh blueberries
4 large strawberries with caps

❀ Prepare 4 dessert plates for use.

❀ Slice each strawberry lengthwise, from the pointed end three-quarters of the way to the cap. Do not remove caps. Fan out the slices.

❀ Peel papayas. Cut in half lengthwise. Scoop out and discard seeds. Place one half on each dessert plate.

❀ Fill papaya halves with longans, kiwis, raspberries and blueberries, allowing a few extra pieces of fruit to spill over onto plate. Top each with a strawberry fan. Spoon 1 - 2 tablespoons reserved longan syrup over the fruits and serve.

Serves 4

NOTE: Papaya is a pear-shaped fruit that can weigh anywhere from ½ to 20 pounds. The most commonly available papayas in supermarkets weigh about 1 pound each and can be either yellow-skinned or green-skinned. The flesh of the yellow-skinned papaya is usually yellow; the flesh of the green-skinned papaya is orange. They are interchangeable. A papaya is ready to eat if it feels soft when pressed. Select fruit with clean, smooth skin that is free of soft spots and bruises.

Berries in Plum Wine

1 cup fresh blackberries
1 cup fresh red raspberries
1 cup fresh blueberries
1 cup sliced strawberries
juice from 1 blood orange
2 tablespoons plum wine or to taste
sugar or honey to taste

❀   In a large bowl, combine berries, orange juice and plum wine. Add sugar to taste. Refrigerate at least 1 hour. Serve.

Serves 4

Variations on the Theme

Citrus Fruits in Plum Wine

Substitute: *1 pomelo, 2 - 3 oranges, 2 - 3 blood oranges, 1 pink grapefruit and 1 Ugli* for the *berries.*
Add*: lime slices* for garnish.
❀   Section the fruits. Cut pomelo and grapefruit sections into 2 or 3 smaller pieces.
❀   Garnish with slices of lime.

Plums in Plum Wine

Substitute: *1 - 2 cups each of sliced red, black and green plums* for the *berries.*
Add: *mint leaves* for garnish

Melons in Plum Wine

Substitute*: cantaloupe, honeydew and watermelon* for the *berries.* Cut melons into chunks or make into balls.
❀   Alternate melon balls or chunks on 4" frilled toothpicks.

TROPICAL FRUIT CUP

1 - 2 ripe mangoes Peel. Cut flesh into small cubes. Discard seeds.
1 papaya Peel. Scoop out and discard seeds. Cut flesh into small cubes.
1 - 2 pounds fresh lichees Peel lichees, starting at stem ends. Halve the translucent, white flesh and remove it from the seed (do this over a bowl to catch any juice). Discard the seeds.
4 kiwis Peel. Cut 3 into chunks. Cut 1 into crosswise slices and reserve.
3 sweet carambolas (star fruit) Cut 2 into chunks. Cut 1 into thin crosswise slices and reserve.

❀   In a large bowl, combine mangoes, papaya, lichees, kiwi chunks and carambola chunks. Refrigerate 1 hour to blend juices.

❀   Spoon fruits mixture into small bowls. Garnish with reserved kiwi and carambola slices. Serve.

Serves 6 - 8

NOTE: Lichees, also spelled litchi and lychee, are about the size and shape of large strawberries with thin, somewhat leathery, bumpy skin. Freshly picked lichees have red skin which turns to brown very quickly. The lichees we see in stores are more brown than red. As long as the skin is dry to the touch, the fruit is good. Avoid fruits that feel slimy and look moldy.

VARIATIONS ON THE THEME

Fresh lichees unavailable?
Substitute: *1 15-ounce can lichees including juice.*
Add: *1 15-ounce can longans including juice.*

MINTED MELON BALLS

2 - 3 cups honeydew balls
2 - 3 cups cantaloupe balls
2 - 3 cups red watermelon balls
2 - 3 cup yellow watermelon balls
½ cup coarsely chopped fresh mint leaves or to taste

❀   In a large bowl, combine melon balls and mint. Serve.

Serves 6 - 8

NOTE: If making melon balls ahead of time, keep watermelon balls in a separate container to maintain the fresh taste and flavor of watermelon. Add to honeydew and cantaloupe balls just before serving.

VARIATION ON THE THEME

MINTED MELON BALLS WITH LICHEES

Add: *1 15-ounce can lichees* to melon balls.
❀   Alternate melon balls and lichees on 4" frilled toothpicks.

PERSIMMON SHERBET

(This recipe requires advance preparation)

4 frozen Fuyu persimmons (see note on p.179)

❀   Remove and discard persimmon caps. Cut away and discard a thin layer of skin and flesh from the cap end. Cover frozen persimmons with plastic wrap. Leave in the refrigerator for 2 - 3 hours to partially thaw.

❀   Place partially thawed persimmons in small shallow bowls. With a teaspoons, diners will scoop out the delicious sherbet from the skin. Persimmon sherbet—an elegant yet simple dessert.

Serves 4

AUTUMN FRUITS WITH HONEY & LIME

1 Red Delicious apple or other red apple
1 Golden Delicious apple
1 Anjou pear
1 Bosc pear
1 - 2 limes or to taste, juiced
1 - 2 tablespoons honey or to taste

❀   Core apples and pears. Cut into wedges or chunks. Toss with lime juice and honey to taste. Serve.

Serves 4

HOW TO STEAM

Equipment you will need:

A STEAMER BASE. This can be a wok, a Dutch oven, a large frying pan with a dome lid or the base that comes with a steamer set.

STEAMER RACK or BASKET. This can be a perforated rack made especially to fit into a wok. Lacking that, you can put 4 bamboo chopsticks (arranged in tic-tac-toe fashion) in a wok or put 3 tuna fish cans opened at both ends in a Dutch oven or frying pan, and place a cake rack on top. Bamboo steamer baskets can be placed directly in a wok. Metal steamer baskets usually come with their own bases.

A COVER. This should be tight-fitting. Use wok cover, pot cover or the cover that comes with a steamer set.

TO STEAM: Bring water in steamer base to a boil. Place food on the steamer rack or in the steamer basket. Cover. Set timer for required time.

Steaming is cooking food with moist heat. Food to be steamed can be placed directly on a lined or unlined steamer rack or on a heat-proof plate or bowl. Make sure the plate or bowl used is at least ½" smaller (all around) than the steamer tier or steamer rack to allow free movement of the steam. Remember the steam must reach the food to cook it.

Water in the steamer base or wok should not touch the food being steamed. The surface of the water should be at least 1" (preferably 2") away from the bottom of the steamer rack or steamer basket.

If a steamer base cannot hold sufficient water to cook the food for the prescribed length of time, have a kettle of boiling water ready to replenish the steamer when the water level gets low. You will need to increase the cooking time by a few minutes each time you open the steamer.

Always start counting your steaming time after the water in the steamer has come to a boil.

GLOSSARY OF INGREDIENTS

BABY CORN: Miniature corn-on-the-cob. Can be eaten as is from the can. Varies in size from 2 - 3" long. Unused corn should be immersed in cold water and refrigerated. Will keep up to 7 days if water is changed daily.

BAMBOO SHOOTS: In this book, refers to canned bamboo shoots packed in water. Available in various size cans: whole, half & chunk, sliced or shredded. Unused bamboo shoots should be immersed in cold water and refrigerated. Will keep up to 7 days if water is change daily.

BEAN SAUCE: A thick, brown, salty paste made from soybeans. Comes in two forms: regular (some of the beans are left whole) and ground. Packed in cans or bottles. Once opened, canned bean sauce should be transferred to a non-corrosive container with a tight fitting lid. Store bottled bean sauce in its original container. Both types will keep indefinitely in the refrigerator.

BEAN SPROUTS: There are two kinds of bean sprouts sold in Asian stores: soybean sprouts and mung bean sprouts. In this book, refers to the mung bean sprouts, which are also the type sold in supermarkets.

BEAN THREAD: See p.149.

BLACK BEANS, FERMENTED: See fermented black beans.

BLOOD ORANGE: A sweet orange with orange-red skin, and flesh ranging from rust to garnet. Juice has a rich citrus flavor and a raspberrylike aftertaste. Use as you would use any oranges in fruit salad or as a garnish.

BOK CHOY, REGULAR: Also spelled bak choi or baicai. A non-heading variety of Chinese cabbage. Regular bok choy is 12" or more in length, with long, white, tender stalks and green, oval leaves.

BOK CHOY, BABY: A shorter version of regular bok choy, 6 - 8" in length. Has a finer texture and a sweeter taste than regular bok choy.

BOK CHOY, SHANGHAI: Similar to baby bok choy, except the stalks are pale green with a bulbous base.

CALABAZA: Also called West Indian pumpkin or Cuban squash. A pumpkin with bright orange, fine-grained, sweet flesh. Use as you would use pumpkin.

CARAMBOLA: Also known as star fruit because its crosswise slices are star-shaped. There are two kinds of carambolas: sweet and sour. Those available in supermarkets are usually sweet carambolas. Select firm, juicy-looking, golden yellow fruits that have a nice fruity aroma.

CHAYOTE: Also known as mirliton. A 4 - 6" pear-shaped squash with pale green or white skin. Cut in half lengthwise to remove the seed. Use peeled, or unpeeled, as you would use summer squash.

CHILI OIL, ASIAN: Also called red pepper oil or hot oil. Made from hot red chili peppers and sesame or vegetable oil. Store at room temperature.

CHILI PEPPERS, FRESH: Range from mild to very, very hot. Size has no bearing on the heat. The tiny pequin is very, very hot. Do not touch your eyes or other sensitive areas of your face when handling chili peppers. Wash hands immediately after handling or wear gloves if possible.

CHILI SAUCE, ASIAN: A thick red sauce made from hot red chili peppers. There are many brands on the market. Try different brands to find one you like. Will keep indefinitely in the refrigerator.

CHILI SAUCE, ASIAN GARLIC: Asian chili sauce with garlic added. Asian chili garlic sauce and Asian chili sauce are interchangeable.

CHINESE BROCCOLI: See gai lan.

CHINESE CELERY: More aromatic and less compact than regular celery. Stalks are round (about the thickness of a pencil) but flat at the base and less than ½" wide. If unavailable, substitute regular celery.

CHINESE CHIVES: Also known as garlic chives. Has flat, bright green leaves ¼" wide and 6 - 9" long. Has a delicate garlic flavor. The flower stems, including buds, are also edible. If unavailable, substitute scallions.

CHINESE EGG NOODLES: See p. 148 under Wheat Noodles.

CHINESE EGGPLANT: Sweeter than regular eggplant and have a silky texture. Long and slender with pale violet skin that is thin and tender and never needs peeling. If unavailable, substitute Japanese eggplant.

CHINESE HAM: There are two kinds of Chinese ham: Kin Hwa ham and Yunnan Ham. They are interchangeable. If unavailable, substitute any dry-cured ham.

CHINESE KALE: See choy sum.

CHINESE LONG BEANS: Also known as yard-long beans. There are two varieties: green and white. The green variety has a firm, crisp texture; the white variety has a softer texture. They are interchangeable.

CHINESE PANCAKES: These are wafer-thin pancakes made from flour and water. Available frozen in Asian markets.

CHINESE PARSLEY: Also known as cilantro or coriander. An herb with an aroma and flavor all its own. Has flat, lacy, green leaves . Both leaves and stems are used. The roots can also be used in cooking.

CHINESE RED VINEGAR: See vinegar, Chinese red.

CHINESE ROCK SUGAR: Irregularly shaped chunks of white to pale-gold sugar.

Made from a combination of honey, maltose and raw sugar. Frequently used in braising. Gives finished dishes a glaze and gravy a rich flavor. Also used to sweeten tea. Store at room temperature in an airtight container. Will keep indefinitely.

CHINKIANG VINEGAR: See vinegar, Chinkiang.

CHOY SUM: Also referred to as Chinese kale. A member of the cabbage family, has long stems and yellow flowers. Considered by many as the best of the Chinese cabbages. Broccoli rabe makes a good substitute.

CLOUD EARS: Also known as tree ears. A fungus that grows on tree. Sold dry, they are irregularly shaped, black on one side and a shade lighter on the other and about the thickness of thumbnail. (Not to be confused with that cousin, wood ears, which are much larger and thicker and black on one side and near white and fuzzy on the other.) After soaking, cloud ears swell to 2 - 3 times its dry form. Has a crunchy and slightly rubbery texture. Will keep indefinitely at room temperature.

CURRY POWDER: A blend of different spices. Typical ingredients are: coriander seeds, cumin, chilies, tumeric, cinnamon, ginger. Can be purchased from Asian markets or supermarkets.

DAIKON: Also known as Chinese radish. A long (12" or more) white, carrot-shaped root vegetable that belongs to the same family as red radish. Daikon is relatively mild and very crisp. Select roots that are heavy with no soft spots.

DRIED SHRIMP: Precooked, shelled and dried shrimp. Quite salty. The taste is concentrated, so a little goes a long way. Comes in various sizes. Stored at room temperature in an airtight container, will keep indefinitely.

FERMENTED BLACK BEANS: Also called salted black beans or preserved beans. These dry, soft, salty beans are made from black soybeans. Some have ginger slices added, and others are seasoned with five-spice powder. Packaged in a plastic bag or cardboard container. Stored at room temperature in an air-tight, non-corrosive container, will keep indefinitely.

FIVE-SPICE POWDER: A brown powder made from a blend of star anise, cloves, Sichuan (Szechuan) peppercorns, fennel and Chinese cinnamon. Store at room temperature, away from heat, light and moisture, in a container (preferably glass) with a tight-fitting lid. Good as long as it retains its aroma.

FIVE-SPICE PRESSED TOFU: See page 106.

FUZZY MELON: Looks like a chubby cucumber covered with white stubble. A member of the winter melon family, fuzzy melon could be called Chinese summer squash as it is used in much the same manner as Western summer squash. Select small green fuzzy melons that are heavy and firm.

GAI LAN: Also known as Chinese broccoli. A member of the cabbage family. A leafy vegetable with white flowers and smooth fat stems (½ - ¾" in diameter). Select thick stalks with green unblemished leaves and more of the white flowers in bud than in bloom.

GINGER: A knobby, beige-brown rhizome with thin dry skin. Fresh ginger can be purchased in two forms: young and mature. Young ginger (not available all year) is tender and fiber-free with a mild flavor; mature ginger is fibrous with a more pungent flavor. Select ginger with smooth unwrinkled skin.

GLUTINOUS RICE: See page 139.

HO FUN: See page 149 under rice noodles.

HOISIN SAUCE: A thick, dark, brownish-red soybean-based sauce with a slightly sweet and spicy taste. Sold in cans or jars. Once opened,canned hoisin sauce should be transferred to a non-corrosive container with a tight-fitting lid. Store bottled hoisin sauce in its original container. Will keep indefinitely in the refrigerator.

HONG KONG-STYLE NOODLES: See page 148 under wheat noodles.

JICAMA: Also known as yam bean. A tuber that looks like a big turnip with sandy-brown skin. Peel away the skin to reveal sweet, crispy, white flesh. If there is also a thin layer of white fibrous flesh under the skin, remove it. Jicama can be eaten cooked or uncooked. Frequently used as a substitute for water chestnuts and bamboo shoots. Select jicama that is firm and heavy.

KABOCHA: A turban-shaped, green-skinned pumpkin with a sweet fiber-free flesh. Used as you would pumpkin and winter squash. Select fruit that is heavy for its size, with clean, unblemished skin.

KAN SSU: See page 106 about tofu.

KIN HWA HAM: Also spelled Jinhua ham. See Chinese ham.

KOHLRABI: A swollen stem that looks like a turnip with leaves. Skin ranges from light green to purplish. The light green variety is more commonly seen in stores. Select kohlrabi that is less than 3" in diameter. The larger ones tend to be woody.

LICHEE: See page 183.

LO MEIN NOODLES: See page 148 under Wheat Noodles.

LONGAN: Literal translation means "dragon eye, a name given probably because of the big, black, shiny seed in the center of the fruit". A relative of the lichee, longan is a round tropical fruit about the size of large olive with thin, light brown skin. To eat, peel away the skin to reveal the translucent, white, juicy pulp. The seed is not edible. Also available canned in heavy syrup.

LOTUS ROOT, FRESH: A tan rhizome that grows underwater and looks like links of very fat sausages. Cut away the nodes at the ends of each section to reveal tunnels that run the entire length of the section. Peel before using, then cut into slices or chunks. Thin cross-sections with their holey, lace-like patterns add elegance to any dish and are frequently used as a garnish. Select hard, whole unblemished roots.

Virtually every part of the lotus plant is used. The leaves are used as a wrapper for steamed food; the seeds are used whole in soup and stews or puréed to make filling for pastries; the seed pods are used in dried flower arrangements. The lotus flower, depicted in so much Chinese artwork is admired by the Chinese not only for its beauty but also as a symbol of the rebirth of humankind.

MANGO: Oval or round in shape, ranging in size as small as a golf ball to as large as a fist, and ranging in color from green to golden with or without tinges of red. A ripe mango has a pleasant smell and feels soft when pressed lightly. Do not judge the ripeness of a mango by the color of its skin as some varieties remain green when ripe.

MEE FUN: See page 149 under Rice Noodles.

MEIN JIN: See page 106.

MISO: A paste made from fermented soybeans. One of the basic ingredients in Japanese cuisine. Comes in various colors and textures. The miso used in this book as a substitute for Chinese bean sauce is the brown, smooth kind.

MUSHROOMS, CHINESE DRIED: Also known as doong goo, black mushrooms or shiitake mushrooms. There are two varieties available in Asian markets. The most common and least expensive variety, hsiang goo (fragrant mushroom), has black caps and tan gills and is sold, with or without stems, in plastic bags. The other variety, hwa goo (flower mushroom), has a patterned cap, with tan fissures running through a dark background. After soaking, hwa goo nearly doubles in thickness. Cooked hwa goo has a plush, chewy texture that is very satisfying. Occasionally sold in plastic bags, but usually packaged in fancy boxes. Expensive but worth it.

MUSHROOMS, ENOKI: White mushrooms with spaghetti-like stems that are bunched together at the base, and tiny caps. Select mushrooms with white caps and stems. Avoid enoki with slimy-looking caps and/or watery stems.

MUSHROOMS, STRAW: In this book, refers to canned straw mushrooms. There are two kinds of canned straw mushrooms: peeled and unpeeled. Both come in small, medium and large. All are interchangeable. Immerse any unused portions in water and refrigerate. Change water daily. Will keep up to 3 days.

NAPA CABBAGE: A heading variety of Chinese cabbage. A short, fat cabbage with wide stems and broad thin leaves. Milder and more tender than regular cabbage, but with a higher water content. Select heads that are white, fresh-looking, firm, heavy and free of wilted leaves and soft spots.

NOODLES, CHINESE EGG: See page 148 under Wheat Noodles.

OYSTER SAUCE: A salty, brown sauce made from oyster extract and spices. Sold in bottles or cans. Bottled oyster sauce should be kept in its original container. Once opened, canned oyster sauce should be transferred to a non-corrosive container with a tight-fitting lid. Will keep indefinitely in the refrigerator.

PACIFIC CLAMS: These are canned, ready-to-eat small clams. Tender and tasty.

PAPAYA: See page 181.

PERSIMMONS: See page 179.

PINE NUTS: Also known as pignolo, pignon, pignolia or pinocchio nuts. The seeds from the cones of the Roman or stone pine. Pine nuts are sold already shelled. Because of the unstable resinous oils they contain, pine nuts become rancid very easily. Use as soon as purchased. For longer storage, keep in the freezer.

PLUM WINE: A sweet wine made from plums. Available in liquor stores.

POMELO: Also spelled pummelo. Also known as shaddock or Chinese grapefruit. Somewhat pear-shaped, can range in size from a bit larger than grapefruit to basket-ball size. The skin is quite thick and is used in cooking. The flesh ranges from white to pink-red. Select fruit that is heavy for its size with skin that looks plump.

RED BEAN CURD: Also called preserved bean curd. Fermented bean curd pre-served in brine with wine and red rice added. The moist, creamy texture and pun-gent aroma of red bean curd is like that of a strong soft cheese. Sold in jars or crocks. Will keep indefinitely in the refrigerator.

RICE: See page 139.

RICE NOODLES: See page 149.

RICE STICKS: See page 149 under Rice Noodles.

RICE WINE: Made of rice and water. If unavailable substitute pale dry sherry.

SESAME OIL, ASIAN: An amber-colored oil made from toasted sesame seeds. Has a strong, rich, nutty, aroma and flavor. Not interchangeable with sesame seed oil sold in health food stores, which is made from untoasted sesame seeds. Store at room temperature. Will keep up to 1 year.

SESAME SEEDS: Can be either black or white. There is no difference in taste between the two which are interchangeable in cooking. White sesame seeds are available hulled or unhulled. To prevent sesame seeds from becoming rancid, store in the freezer. Will keep up to 1 year.

SESAME SEED PASTE: A thick, dark brown paste covered with sesame oil. Made from toasted sesame seeds. Not interchangeable with tahini (sesame seed paste used in Middle Eastern cuisine), which is made from untoasted sesame seed.

SHALLOTS: A member of the onion family. Look like clumps of petite onions with reddish-brown skin. Can be eaten raw or cooked.

SHANGHAI BOK CHOY: See BOK CHOY, SHANGHAI.

SHIITAKE MUSHROOMS: See MUSHROOMS, CHINESE DRIED.

SICHUAN PEPPERCORNS: Also called flower pepper because of the reddish-brown open pods. Mildly spicy, the pods have a slight numbing effect on the tongue when chewed. Stored in an airtight container, good as long as it retains its aroma.

SICHUAN PRESERVED VEGETABLES: The knobby root end of a member of the cabbage family preserved with chili powder, salt and spices. Light green or light tan and covered with red chili paste. Crunchy, salty and spicy, tastes like spicy sauerkraut. Sold shredded or whole in cans. Unused portions should be transferred to non-corrosive container with a tight fitting lid. Will keep indefinitely in the refrigerator.

SILK SQUASH: See SZE GWA.

SNOW PEAS: Also called Chinese pea pods. Two varieties are available: the familiar flat variety and the round variety, also known as sugar snap peas or sugar pod peas. The whole pod is eaten. Select snow peas with green, unblemished pods that are crisp and fresh-looking.

SNOW PEA SHOOTS: These are the tender shoots of snow pea plants. A rather expensive and scarce vegetable unless you grow your own. Regular pea shoots can also be used. Keep in mind that by harvesting the pea shoots you are preventing the plants from flowering and producing peas.

SOY SAUCE, DARK: See SOY SAUCE, REGULAR. Because it contains molasses, dark soy sauce is darker, slightly thicker and a little sweeter than regular soy sauce. Will keep indefinitely at room temperature.

SOY SAUCE, MUSHROOM: Dark soy sauce flavored with mushrooms.

SOY SAUCE, REGULAR: A salty, dark liquid made from soybeans. Contains wheat. If you want to use soy sauce but are allergic to wheat, try using tamari. The sodium content of different brands of soy sauce will vary. The recipes in this book were tested using Chinese soy sauce.

STAR ANISE: An eight-seeded star-shaped pod. Has a licorice-like flavor. Store at room temperature in a container with a tight-fitting lid. Good as long as it retains its aroma.

STRAW MUSHROOMS: See mushrooms, straw.

SUGAR SNAP PEAS: See snow peas.

SUNCHOKE: Also known as Jerusalem artichoke. A member of the sunflower family, brown skinned tuber that looks like fresh ginger. The flesh is white and crispy. Can be eaten raw or cooked. Use as you would use potatoes.

SZE GWA: Also known as silk squash, angled luffa or Chinese okra. A member of the gourd family, sze gwa looks like an English cucumber with ridges. Select dark green fruits with tender ridges.

SZECHUAN PEPPERCORNS: See Sichuan peppercorns.

SZECHUAN PRESERVED VEGETABLES: See Sichuan preserved vegetables.

TANGERINE PEEL, DRIED: Sold in Asian markets. Stored in an airtight container, will keep indefinitely at room temperature.

TEA: See page 173.

TERIYAKI SAUCE: Soy sauce flavored with wine, vinegar and other spices and seasonings.

TIANJIN GREEN BEAN STARCH SHEET: See page 149, under Bean Noodles.

TOFU: See page 106.

UGLI: Very sweet and juicy citrus fruit. Use as you would use oranges.

VINEGAR, CHINESE RED: Usually used as a condiment. Cider vinegar makes a good substitute.

VINEGAR, CHINKIANG: Also known as brown vinegar. Actually more black than brown. Made from glutinous rice, it has a sweet fragrance and tart, distinctive flavor similar to balsamic vinegar. Sold in bottles. Will keep indefinitely at room temperature.

VINEGAR, RICE: Actually all Chinese vinegars are made from rice. When a recipe calls for rice vinegar, it usually refers to the light yellow or white rice vinegar.

WATER CHESTNUT: A small, round, edible root, with a pointed top and brown-black skin. After peeling, reveals off-white flesh that is sweet and crunchy. Canned water chestnuts are used in this book. When fresh ones are available, feel free to substitute; they are quite different in flavor and texture than the canned ones.

WINTER MELON: A member of the gourd family. A mature winter melon is about the size of watermelon. Has a hard, green skin covered with a dusting of white powder. Commonly sold by the slice. Should have plump, firm, white flesh and a clean smell.

WONTON WRAPPERS: Also called wonton skin. A 3½" square noodle dough made from wheat flour, egg and water. Fresh wrappers are smooth and pliable and easy to work with. Sold in 1-pound packages wrapped in moisture-proof paper. Fresh wonton wrappers will keep for one week in the refrigerator. Freeze for longer storage. Wonton wrappers sold in Asian markets come in various thicknesses. The one I prefer is labeled "Thin Wonton Skin" and has about 90 wrappers to a pound. The ones sold in supermarkets are much thicker.

YUNNAN HAM: See Chinese ham.

LIST OF INGREDIENTS

Due to the many dialects of Chinese, an ingredient, because of different regional pronunciations, can end up with different spellings when transliterated in English. To further complicate matters, different manufacturers will frequently use different English names for the same ingredient.

Then there is mistranslation. An example is "Red Bean Curd." On the bottle of one manufacturer's label the English reads "Bean Sauce" but the Chinese reads "Red Bean Curd." Not to mention the fact that red bean curd and bean sauce are two entirely different ingredients.

The following list has helped my students (those who do not read Chinese) in their shopping expeditions. I hope it will help you too.

Make a copy of the list and bring it with you whenever you go shopping for Chinese ingredients.

BAMBOO SHOOTS, SHREDDED 竹筍絲

BEAN SAUCE, REGULAR 原晒豉

BEAN THREAD 粉絲

BOK CHOY, BABY 小白菜

BOK CHOY, SHANGHAI 上海白菜

CHILI OIL 辣油 or 青棟菜

CHILI SAUCE 辣椒醬

CHILI GARLIC SAUCE 蒜辣椒醬

CHINESE CELERY 芹菜

CHINESE CHIVES 韮菜

CHINESE EGGPLANT 矮瓜

CHINESE HAM 火腿

CHINESE LONG BEANS 豆角

CHINESE PANCAKES 薄餅

CHINESE PARSLEY 芫茜 or 香菜

CHINESE ROAST PORK 义燒

CHINESE ROCK SUGAR 冰糖

CHOY SUM 菜心

CLOUD EARS 云耳

DAIKON 蘿蔔

DRIED SHRIMP 虾米

EGG NOODLES, FRESH 新鮮蛋麵

FERMENTED BLACK BEANS 豆豉

FIVE-SPICE POWDER 五香粉

FUZZY MELON 節瓜 or 毛瓜

GAI LAN 芥蘭

GLUTINOUS RICE 糯米

HOISIN SAUCE 海鮮醬

KAN SSU 干絲

LICHEE 荔枝

LICHEE TEA 荔枝紅茶

LONGAN 龍眼

LOTUS ROOT 蓮藕

MEIN JIN 麵筋

MUSHROOMS: HSIANG GOO 香菇

HWA GOO 花菇

NAPA CABBAGE 天津白菜

OYSTER SAUCE 蠔油

PACIFIC CLAMS 珍珠鮑貝

PINE NUTS 松子

RED BEAN CURD 南乳

RICE NOODLES, DRIED 干河粉

RICE NOODLES, FRESH 沙河粉

RICE STICKS 米粉

RICE WINE 紹興酒

SESAME OIL 蔴油

SESAME SEEDS, BLACK 黑芝蔴

SESAME SEEDS, WHITE 白芝蔴

SICHUAN PRESERVED VEGETABLES 四川榨菜

SICHUAN PEPPERCORN 四川花椒

SNOW PEAS SHOOTS 豆苗

SOY SAUCE, DARK 老抽

SOY SAUCE, MUSHROOM 草菰老抽

SOY SAUCE, REGULAR 生抽

STAR ANISE 八角

STRAW MUSHROOMS 草菇

SZE GWA 絲瓜

TANGERINE PEEL, DRIED 陳皮

TIANJIN GREEN BEAN STARCH SHEET 天津粉皮

TOFU, FIVE-SPICE PRESSED 五香豆付干 or 上海五香干

TOFU, FIRM 老豆付

TOFU, SOFT 嫩豆付

VINEGAR, CHINKIANG 鎮江香醋

VINEGAR, RED 紅浙醋

VINEGAR, RICE 米醋

WINTER MELON 冬瓜

WONTON WRAPPERS 雲吞皮

INDEX

C

NOTES